Conflict Resolution

Concepts and Practice

By Marcus Goncalves

ASME Press   ◆   New York

Library of Congress Cataloging-in-Publication Data

Gonτalves, Marcus.
  Conflict resolution : concepts and practice / by Marcus Goncalves.
    p. cm.
  Includes bibliographical references.
  ISBN 978-0-7918-0274-8
  1. Conflict management. I. Title.
  HD42.G65 2008
  658.3'145--dc22
                                    2008009810

Who Should Read This Book

This book is primarily designed for those who are or plan to be involved with conflict resolution, as well as for anyone interested or immersed in such process; for project and team leaders and managers, or anyone performing in those roles or soon to be performing in those roles.

Table of Contents

Chapter 5

Dedication

To my forever beautiful wife Carla, and my three children Samir (living here on earth), Josh and Andrea (living in Heaven). These are the real treasures of my life.

To God be the glory!

Marcus Goncalves

Acknowledgment

So many people helped during the process of writing this book, it is impossible to keep track of them all. To all that I have forgotten to list, please don't hold it against me! First and foremost are the members of the faculty and the Management Department at Nichols College. They have made Nichols an enjoyable place to work and to research.

Many thanks (again!) to Mary Grace Stefanchik, the editor at the American Society of Mechanical Engineers (ASME), for not only inviting me to write another book for ASME's collection, but especially for her patience with me, for my busy schedule; to professor Vijay Kanabar, at Boston University for his great friendship, professionalism, and unconditional support. I also would like to thank James Willey, VP of Covanta Energy of Philippines, for entrusting me to test many of my methods and providing valuable feedback; professor Kip Becker, Ph.D., Chairman, Department of Administrative Sciences at Boston University; for his unconditional support.

I would also like to express my appreciation to many corporate leaders that shared their views and experiences with me about conflict resolution. My special thanks go to the following leaders: Leslie Field, at Siemens, NJ; Semih Arslanoglu, at Intel Corp.; Mark Payne, at International Paper in U.S.; and Sybil Smith, Executive Director of Graduate Studies at Rabb School, Brandeis University.

Many thanks also go to my spiritual partners at the Boston Church of Christ, Steve Major and Matt Paradise, for their continuous spiritual support and friendship. Last but not least, my deepest gratitude to my wife Carla, sons Samir and Josh (in memory), and my princess Andrea (also in memory), the true joy of my life. I could not forget Ninigapa (my parakeet), Gus (our Cocker Spaniel), and the new addition to the family, Phoenix, our red bally parrot who greets me every day with a "good morning."

To God be the glory!

Preface

There are several companies today that recognize that if internal conflict can be managed strategically, it will lead to success in the global marketplace--despite multiculturalism and other filters every employee and team member may have. Those that ignore conflict entirely and incur its unnecessary costs will be at a competitive disadvantage. I believe that companies that fail to address conflict as a strategic issue will also be at competitive disadvantage.

In *Conflict Resolution: Concepts and Practice*, you will hopefully find a brief, but insightful overview of the aspects of conflict resolution in organizations. Questions such as what are conflicts, why they happen, how they are formed, how they can be avoided, what are the root causes of conflicts, how to deal with conflicts, and how to mediate conflicts will be answered.

This book is not, however, intended to comprehensively cover the subject. There are a lot of resources available out there and the bibliography may help you in expanding your knowledge on the topic. The idea of this book is to provide you with a good overview on the topic. The book also should serve as a resource companion for those professionals attempting the Engineering Management Certificate International (EMCI) offered by the American Society of Mechanical Engineers (ASME), for which this book was carefully tailored. But, of course, this book can be of great use to any business professionals seeking to develop an effective change management strategy.

The book is broken up into nine chapters covering all the main aspects of the conflict resolution process. There is also a comprehensive list of references and recommended reading at the end of this book. Here it is an overview of the book:

Chapter 1, *Understanding What a Conflict Is*, provides you with an overview of conflict resolution. It discusses what a conflict is, and is not, the aspects of a conflict and triggers at organization's teams and coworkers.

Chapter 2, *Why We Avoid Conflicts?*, provides an insight on the reasons we naturally tend to avoid conflicts, its multidimensional aspects and basic understanding on dealing with conflicts and conflict styles we adopt.

Chapter 3, *The Root Cause of Conflicts*, provides a more in-depth discussion on the major causes of conflict, how to detect and deal with them, and the impacts it exercises at organizations. This chapter also discusses conflict transformation and the role of perceptions in a conflict.

Chapter 4, *The Path Through and Out of Conflicts*, shows how important it is to understand the main conflict resolution styles, the role of perceptions and communication in resolving conflicts, and the role of leadership in addressing, mediating and preventing conflicts.

Chapter 5, *The Role of Perceptions and the Six Stages of Conflict Resolution*, is an in-depth discussion on the role of perceptions during conflict resolution and negotiation, bringing a pragmatic approach to conflict resolution.

Chapter 6, *Conflict Mediation*, expands on previous chapters discussing conflict resolution strategies by identifying and describing the role of a conflict mediator, and the various aspects of mediation, including the distinction between mediation and arbitration.

Chapter 7, *Negotiating Conflicts*, offers a discussion on how to negotiate agreements during the process of conflict resolution, looking at how to determine the best alternative to negotiate agreements and other important aspects of the process.

Chapter 8, *Conflict Resolution Best Practices*, provides a brief overview of the best practices aspects in conflict resolution. This chapter is drawn on practical experience on conflict dynamics, leadership and communication skills in working with teams and leading organizations.

Chapter 9, *Test Yourself: Are You a Good Conflict Mediator*, provides you with an opportunity to assess your conflict resolution and mediation skills and the areas you must develop to become a better mediator or self-mediator. This is a simple, but effective self-test to measure your skills in dealing with conflicts.

At the end of the book there is a section proving you with a comprehensive list of references and recommended readings on the topic of conflict resolution.

Chapter 1
Understanding Conflicts

The art of conflict resolution is highly dependent on the ability to get to the right depth of understanding and intervention in conflict[1].

Overview

Some people love to be in a conflict. If this applies to you, then you better close this book and look for another one, as this book is for those people that do not like to be in conflicts, but rather like to solve them. Some people face conflicts head-on, while others tend to avoid such situations by running away from them. These people don't wait for any signs, nor look for prizes.

Many of us believe that conflicts are natural, inevitable, necessary, and normal. Many also believe that the problem with conflicts is not the existence of differences, but how we handle it. Nonetheless, many of us tend to be unwilling to admit when we are in the midst of conflict. Many business professionals are quick to assure their peers and co-workers that the fierce argument they are having with regard to a product or service is not a conflict, but just a "discussion." Corporate America spends millions of dollars hiring facilitators to guide it in strategic planning, goal-setting, quality circles, team building, and all manner of training, but is not so willing to hire conflict resolution trainers and mediators to ask for help when internal conflicts arise.

As part of my management consulting practice at MGCG, we tend to be involved in many operational and strategic projects, but very few conflict-resolution ones. Very few honest and brave executives are willing to ask us for training on preventive conflict approaches, or to mediate a conflict. The perception is that to convey

---

[1] Bernard S. Mayer, *The Dynamics of Conflict Resolution: A Practitioner's Guide*

1

that there is a conflict is to admit a failure and to concede the existence of a situation that is doomed to failure.

This ambivalence about conflict is rooted in the same primary challenge conflict resolvers face - coming to terms with the nature of conflict. Conflict resolution is an art and a science. It is about teaching professionals, and people in general, new ways to work through and resolve disputes that do not involve physical violence. Many business organizations offer conflict resolution programs for its employees. When dealing with conflicts, people may think of it on many different levels, and how we view a conflict will greatly determine our wiliness, attitude and approach in dealing with the issue at hand.

We all would like to think that business affairs are essentially rational, that they work like any other tangible interaction in this world, and that we should therefore be able to gain from these interactions. However, we just need to take a look at the financial section of any newspaper, the TV news, the financial bulletins or even Wall Street to realize that business, particularly in the twenty-first century, is anything but rational.

Why Think About Conflict?

The premise of this book is that conflict and conflict resolution are useful areas of focus in business, and in any creative and innovative process. Conflict is actually not a bad human dynamic. There are several reasons that justify it as necessary for the growth and development of professionals, teams, and organizations. Conflict can help build teams, defining and balancing coworkers' needs as professionals with their needs as participants in the larger organization, or corporation. In addition, working through a conflict can be an important bonding and growth-producing experience. The strength of corporate systems (policies and procedures), as well as social systems, lies in part in how they prevent serious conflicts and, when conflicts do arise, how they address them so as to maintain system integrity and preserve the wellbeing of their members. By facing major conflicts, addressing them, reorganizing as necessary to deal with them, and moving on, teams and organizations adapt to changes in their environment. Understanding the dynamics of conflict therefore provides conflict resolution professionals with a basic tool for addressing the essential forces that shape the development of professionals, teams, and the organization as a whole.

It is easy enough to say that conflict is inevitable and is not in itself good or bad, yet for many people, accepting this premise is an uphill battle. There may be an important lesson for us in the resistance that people have to acknowledging conflict in their lives. This may be something other than dysfunctional conflict-avoidant behavior. Maybe there is an inevitable shift in the way people interact with each other once they acknowledge the presence of conflict, and therefore have good reason to approach that admission with caution. If this shift in focus, energy, attitude, or behavior is a natural consequence of the emergence of conflict, and if conflict is itself necessary, inevitable, and often healthy, this poses a fundamental dilemma for all of us as individuals existing in groups. We had therefore better strive to comprehend the nature of conflict in all its complexities. Understanding conflict becomes the vehicle for understanding the many contradictions that are necessarily present in our efforts to be social beings.

Furthermore, there is always something that can be done about conflict. This does not mean that it can always be resolved, but a productive response can usually be made to move conflict along a constructive path. At times, this response may be to escalate a conflict so that it emerges into people's consciousness or takes on a higher priority for resolution. Sometimes the response may be to do nothing and let events develop, allowing the conflict to mature. Sometimes it may be to help people understand their needs and express their feelings at a deeper, more meaningful level. Sometimes it may be to find some Band-Aid to stop the bleeding, or to look for creative solutions that all parties can accept. There is no single correct response to conflict, but that does not mean that there are not wise and unwise responses to any particular conflict. Our success as individuals, communities, organizations, and societies is in no small measure related to our developing wisdom about how we can respond to the many conflicts that we face.

Understanding Conflict Resolution

There are many perspectives on conflict, but in general it can be viewed as a feeling, a disagreement, a real or perceived incompatibility of interests, inconsistent worldviews, or a set of behaviors. If you are to efficiently handle a conflict, you must understand its nature. You will also need tools and techniques to help you distinguish the many multifaceted interactions that may compose a conflict, helping you better understand the roots of the conflict, and giving you a reasonable grip on the forces that motivate the behavior of all participants, including yourself.

Poor working relationships, internal and external strife, conflicts, misunderstandings, low productivity, decreased customer satisfaction, lack of referrals, poor communication, and low sales are all symptoms of chaos, all symptoms of gaps that are not being bridged, intentionally or not. The knowledge economy is characterized by constant and fast change, and to be successful organizations and professionals must embrace change as quickly as it comes.

Nonetheless, to prevent chaos, or a proliferation of gaps, executive leaders must embody the science of bridging gaps, of resolving conflicts, of dealing with ever- changing environments and business landscapes, by developing a productive, team-oriented, positive atmosphere where good communication is paramount. In the twenty-first century economy, executives, and the organization as a whole, must not only learn to manage time but manage themselves. Rather than focusing on tasks and time, managers must focus on preserving and enhancing relationships, and on accomplishing results.

Chaos, the end-result of gaps, is a wonderfully evocative word, a formless void of primordial matter, the great deep; or if you prefer, the abyss out of which the cosmos or order of the universe evolved. Can you think of anything better designed to set the creative energies of executives in motion than the challenge of forming order from the chaos eminent in their business or organization?

Very often, we tend to engage in a conflict with a myriad of assumptions about its nature, whether we are aware of them or not. These assumptions are not all negative, and actually can be very helpful to us. But at many times they can work as pre-conceived ideas, as blinders, limiting our ability to understand what lies beneath a conflict and the many alternatives that often exist to deal with the issue. That is why you need frameworks that can help you expand your ability to think about the conflict in such a way that confronts your potential pre-conceptions and assumptions. Such framework should provide you with practical and readily usable techniques to deal with conflicts. And as you develop your ability to understand conflict in an in-depth and proactive way, you enhance your ability to deal with it more effectively, in accordance with your ethical and

4

moral values, thereby promoting harmony and peace within the groups you lead or belong to.

Unfortunately, schools are not teaching managers to deal with conflicts, never mind how to bridge them when they occur. While business is booming, everything is great, but when a hiccup in business operations occurs, then it is doomsday. The problem is that managers, particularly those in the United States and other developed countries, have been accustomed to believe the familiar bromides. When a manager, or any leader or executive, believes that their responsibilities can be discharged adequately by attending seminars or following simplistic formulas, then we have a problem. When such formulas fail them, not only do they get discouraged and frustrated, sometimes they totally derail.

What is it about the twenty-first century economy that seems so chaotic and full of conflict to executives? Is it the sheer volume of information that needs to be absorbed? Is it the lack of quality assurance we have become used to in financial literature and media? Is it uncertainty about the authority of many business concepts and theories – mine included? Is it not knowing what is out there, especially beyond our international borders? Is it the unmanageable number of materials, experts, gurus and consulting practices available when you attempt to seek advice or professional service? Is it lack of expertise, or the difficulty of establishing a business strategy, a business goal, one that you are sure won't get dismissed by the Board? Perhaps it is the ephemeral nature of being an executive in the twenty-first century -- here today, but changed or gone tomorrow? Or is it the dilemma of executives trying to keep up with both business goals and intra-organizational challenges while attempting to provide the best solutions for both the Board and stock holders? Most probably it is many or all of these things.

Although business disagreements are largely beyond the control of anyone, they are part of what generates conflict. The good news is that conflicts can be resolved, or bridged, as I like to say. But no bridges are created equal, and one must build his/her own conflict resolution (bridge) strategy. Further, as Richard Farson so eloquently points out in his book *Management of the Absurd,* [2] "Years ago we talked about 'leadership,' then the byword became 'morale,' then it was 'motivation,' then 'communication,' then 'culture,' then 'quality,' then 'excellence,' then 'chaos,' then back again to

---

[2] 1997, Free Press, NYC.

5

'leadership.' Along the way we were buffeted about by buzzwords like 'zero defect,' 'management by objectives,' 'quality circles,' 'TQM' (Total Quality Management), 'paradigm shift,' 're-engineering,' 'six-sigma,' and now 'knowledge tornado.'" The confused executive, careening from trend to trend, cannot be an effective leader while believing in simplistic formulas and models, mine included. No wonder we experience so much conflict at the workplace: we all come from a different school of thought!

Complexity science suggests that paradoxes (or conflicts) are not problematic. Rather, they create a tension from which creative solutions emerge. This realization can shake someone at the core of his being. Charles Handy (1995), for example, writes that "The important message for me was that there are never any simple or right answers in any part of life. I used to think that there were, or could be. I now see paradoxes everywhere I look. Every coin, I now realize, has at least two sides." [3] Others see the concept of paradox as so important that they now define leadership as essentially the management of paradoxes. Paradoxes are defined as simultaneous or interdependent opposites. There is a lot of paradox in conflicts!

But What is a Conflict?

By definition, as shown in figure 1.1, conflict is the result of a lack of agreement in reaching a common understanding, where the parties involved perceive a threat to their interests or needs. The two most important components of any conflict are the *needs* and *interests* we have at play, as well as the *concerns* that one may perceive from these situations. Such concerns are often triggered by fear, or by the feeling one has no options. We tend to find ourselves in a conflict when we feel that our needs are not being taken into consideration, which generates a degree of concern, varying from very low to very high. If you were to reflect on a past conflict of yours, you will notice that your needs were threatened, or at least you felt that way.

---

[3] "Waiting for the Mountain to Move: Reflections on Work and Life," Jossey-Bass

Figure 1.1 – What is a conflict?

It is not uncommon for minor disagreements to arise in any business environment, be it at a staff meeting, a conference, or when working in teams. Conflict in itself is not bad, as it is typically a result of differences in opinion, which always bring opportunities to learn and innovate. The problem arises when the parties cannot resolve the conflict (and who said a conflict needs to be resolved?), and the incident turns into serious disagreement, often leading to violence -- be it through words, body language or ultimately physical aggression. Conflicts and disagreements are a part of the business environment, but they do not have to end in violence.

As Bernard S. Mayer (2000) would say, "Conflict resolution is a creative, interactive, and fluid process that requires more than a core of knowledge and a set of tools. To be done successfully, it demands of the conflict resolver a constant internal focus and an evolving awareness of the shifts occurring between the parties being helped." "Conflict is part of a continuum that can lead to harassment or violence," said Philip Chard[4], president of NEAS Inc., the 10th-largest employee-assistance program in the United States, in his June address to the 54th annual conference of the Society for Human Resource Management. In his June address to the 54th annual conference of the Society for Human Resource Management, Chard noted that, on

---

[4] (Indianapolis Business Journal, 09/09/2002)

average, 25 percent of a manager's time is spent on conflict-related issues. Even without getting to the stage of an Equal Employment Opportunity Commission or formal grievance filing, unresolved conflict damages morale, decreases productivity and quality, impedes operations, and can drive away top talent.

The genesis of a conflict, which many times can be serious enough to destroy work groups and relationships, affecting tremendously the productivity of any organization, can be narrowed to three major roots. These three roots are often misunderstood, or not recognized:

- **Is there a disagreement?** - When we're in the middle of a disagreement, we are often aware of the levels of difference in the positions of the two (or more) parties involved in the conflict. But there may be quite a difference between true and perceived disagreement. What we perceive in a disagreement is based on our own understanding of the issue at hand, which is always influenced by several factors that dictate who we are, how we think, and what we think, especially about others. Our perceptions are also influenced by our desires, interests and concerns. To dwell, therefore, on a disagreement that is the fruit of our own perceptions can be disastrous. We must seek out the true issues and roots of this disagreement before making any assumptions and, ultimately, decisions about the issue.

- **Parties Involved** - Another factor very important in every disagreement is knowing and understanding the parties involved. There are often disparate pleas in our sense of who is involved in the conflict. People tend to be surprised, and at times even shocked, to learn that they are part of a conflict. It makes no sense to try to resolve a conflict if all the parties involved are not present, or worse, if we don't know who these parties are.

- **Perceived disagreement** - In every conflict, what we perceive as *threat* is just that: a *perceived* threat. We respond to the perceived threat, rather than the true threat we face. While perceptions don't become reality per se, our behavior, feelings, and ongoing responses become modified by that evolving sense of the threat we confront.

Needs, Interests or Concerns

There is a tendency to narrowly define "the problem" as one of substance, task and near-term viability. However, workplace conflicts tend to be far more complex than that, for they involve ongoing relationships with complex, emotional components. Simply stated, there are always procedural and psychological needs to be addressed within a conflict, in addition to the substantive needs that are generally presented, and the durability of these interests and concerns transcends the immediate present situation. Any efforts to resolve conflicts effectively must take these points into account.

So, is this a simple definition of conflict? I think so. But we must respect that within its elegant simplicity lies a complex set of issues to address. It is not surprising, therefore, that the satisfactory resolution of most conflicts can prove so challenging and time consuming.

When Does a Conflict Occur?

We tend to perceive conflict as a consequence of disagreement, when there is a threat to needs, interests or concerns. When we tend to perceive the conflict as a threat our reactions tend to be very emotional. Somehow we believe that our status quo may change, that our job may be affected, that we may miss an opportunity. In these cases it is very important to figure out what is the source of a threat, and try to convey it to the party that we are having a disagreement with.

A conflict may also occur when we misunderstand the source of the issue. We tend to respond to the perception of the situation, as discussed above, not the reality of it. If we feel threatened by a situation or perceive that our needs are not being met, than we may start a conflict. In addition, we often fail to recognize that conflicts are always multidimensional. Not only do they affect us at a physical level, by threatening our status quo, but also at the emotional and professional levels. In addition, the work environment, corporate policies and procedures, clients, and interpersonal relationships may also affect the ability to resolve conflicts.

Another factor which impacts dealing with conflict is the fact that we don't see disagreements as normal. Differences of opinion are almost predictable at the workplace, and should actually be fostered. We don't realize how creative problem-solving strategies are in dealing with conflicts. Therefore, we should never confuse conflict with indecision, disagreement or stress. While these may be causes of conflicts, they do not yet constitute one, and are not best handled by conflict resolution tools.

If we are going to learn how to resolve conflict, then we must understand what a conflict is. Otherwise, one may be using an excellent tool to fix the wrong problem, but not achieving the desired results. Here is a typical list of the symptoms of conflict:

- The source of the issue is interdependent - In other words, the parties involved in the conflict need something from each other and they are vulnerable to those needs. For instance, your supervisor may need you to work overtime tonight, but you have plans to go to the movies.

- Parties are blaming each other - In a typical conflict parties tend to find fault with each other for causing the problem. For instance, your supervisor may blame you for not wanting to work overtime because you don't care about your job or the project at hand. By the same token, you may blame your supervisor for being insensitive and unreasonable for wanting to take advantage of your good will by asking you to stay late.

- Parties are angry - When the parties in the conflict are angry it's because they feel emotionally upset. But in many conflicts, such emotions are carefully hidden. We tend to keep up the appearance of politeness and cordiality so well that our coworkers might not even be able to see that we are emotionally upset. Hidden or not, emotions are always present in conflicts.

- The behavior in the conflict is causing business problems - A conflict always brings job performance and productivity to its knees, due to lack of cooperation. When individuals are engaged in a conflict they are distracted from their work by their own actions. Such emotional reactions, which are caused by the behaviors individuals use as they interact, directly impact job performance.

To summarize, you will know when there is a conflict when two people whose jobs are interdependent are angry at each other, perceive each other as being at fault, and act in such way as to cause problems to the business, such as decreased productivity, absenteeism, negative synergy, and the like. Notice that this definition includes feelings (emotions), perceptions (thoughts) and actions (behaviors). Psychologists consider these three the only dimensions of human experience. Conflicts, therefore, are rooted in all parts of our human nature.

Don't assume, however, that as a manager you are responsible for keeping all of your employees happy. Some problems are up to the individual to resolve. Some differences are benign, even beneficial to the work environment. If you have not thought the situation through thoroughly, it would be smart not to jump into the middle and try to fix it. You may only make it worse.

Analyzing Conflicts

There are six factors you must consider when analyzing a conflict structure:

- **Interdependent** – When analyzing interdependency you want to find out how much each party in a conflict needs each other to act cooperatively, such as to provide resources or to satisfy some need. If the interdependency of the two parties is high, than the cost of not resolving the conflict will likely be very high.

- **How many interested parties** -- It is very important also to find out how many distinct parties, individuals, or groups have interest in how the conflict is resolved. If the conflict brings only two parties, and those parties are individuals and not groups, resolving the issue may be surprisingly easy and fast. As the number and size of parties increases, thereby increasing the number of people to please, hear and understand, the more difficult it becomes to resolve the conflict.

- **Representation** -- Is the source of conflict inherited from an individual or a group? Does each party of a conflict represent all members of the group? Are these constituents present at the discussion and the conflict? Are they personally and directly involved in the process of resolving the conflict? It is much easier to resolve conflicts when we speak for ourselves and do not have to please all members of a group.

Resolutions are easier to attain when they involve a smaller number of individuals.

- **Negotiator authority** -- Who has the authority to negotiate the conflict? Does one party have to negotiate for a whole group or just for themselves? Does the negotiator party have the authority to make decisions without going back to their constituents for approval? If negotiator authority is high, then the solution is easier. If negotiator authority is low, the process of resolving the conflict will take much longer, and may become a lot more difficult.

- **Level of urgency** -- Is it really necessary that a solution be found in the near future, or can it wait? This is important in determining how clearly everyone understands the criticality of a conflict. The more urgent a conflict resolution is, the less likely it will be to satisfy everyone, to be a consensus. For instance, if there is a fire at a power plant, there may not be much time to decide the approach to extinguish the fire. In this case, consensual solutions may be impossible. Whoever has the responsibility for the safety and security of the power plant will have to make the decisions, very likely following policy and procedure, regardless of the agreement of all parties.

- **Communication channels** – Can the parties talk to each other face-to-face in the same room or are they located remotely? It is a lot more difficult to resolve a conflict when the parties are not face-to-face. Their body language and demeanor when communicating is almost entirely lost (one can still pick up on tone of voice, sarcastic comments and so forth). Even worse is when a conflict needs to be resolved through asynchronous technologies such as e-mail, where each party needs to type into the keyboard their issues and concerns, and then wait for a response. Keep in mind that real-time dialogs typically produce far better solutions than virtual meetings and lesser communications channels.

Also keep in mind, as shown in Figure 1.2, that from time to time you will have to deal with conflicts that have been defined by structures such as the ones discussed above. But overall, when dialing with conflicts, you will always have to address issues of personal, interpersonal and structural barriers.

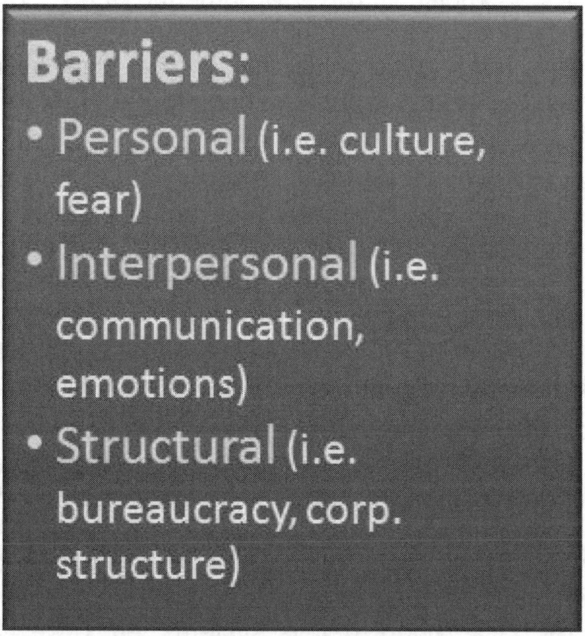

Figure 1.2 - Barriers in dealing with a conflict.

When we talk about personal barriers, remember cultural issues as well as fears. For instance, in the Philippines, where I consulted for a power-generation client, the same issue exists. It became obvious for the local staff, that it would be a lot better to resolve the conflicts among themselves from a Filipino perspective. But when the conflict was multicultural, including an American coworker, the situation was more difficult. This is because the Filipino culture tends to be more passive, and by the same token, the American culture tends to be much more confrontational when in conflict. In this case, the American counterpart was typically in the conflict because of the Filipino counterpart, in order to defend the person in avoiding the conflict altogether.

Although conflict is a normal part of organizational life, providing numerous opportunities for growth through improved understanding and insight, there is a tendency to view conflict as a negative experience caused by abnormally difficult circumstances.

When dealing with the interpersonal aspects of a conflict, such as communication and emotion, the tone, language skills and emotional sensitivity all play an important role in the resolution of the conflict. This is very typical in multicultural environments where coworkers who speak different languages may misunderstand each other. The parties of a conflict tend to perceive that limited alternatives and resources are available in arriving at a solution to the problem, rather than realizing that multiple possibilities may exist.

For instance, identical words in Spanish may have different meanings, depending on which country they are spoken in. I found myself in a difficult situation attempting to resolve a conflict in Costa Rica while referring to a Spanish equivalent of the Ecuador/ Argentina word for *hole*, which my counterpart understood as a completely different word, more specifically a swear. Therefore, be very careful when dealing with workers from different nationalities.

A conflict exceeds the notion of a disagreement, as we perceive it as a threat to our well-being. Conflicts are therefore a significant experience in our lives, to which we must pay attention. Since we tend to respond to a counterpart in a disagreement on the basis of our perceptions of the situation, it is not surprising that we find ourselves in conflicts. Because of our biases (resulting from upbringing, cultural background, beliefs systems, etc.), we filter our perceptions and reactions in a conflict (actually, all the time) through values, information on the issue, experience, gender, and other emotional and physical variables. Our conflict responses, then, become filled with ideas and feelings that can be very powerful catalysts to our perception of the possible solutions available.

Conflicts always contain important and substantive, as well as procedural and psychological, dimensions that must be negotiated. There is no way to achieve a sound solution to a conflict without understanding the threat perceived by those engaged in the conflict. We must consider all of these dimensions, not as extraordinary, but as normal experiences within the work environment. Furthermore, conflicts are, for the most part, predictable and expectable at the workplace, and when working as a team, as depicted in figure 1.3. Such situations tend to arise naturally during complex and stressful projects in which coworkers are significantly invested. It would be wise, therefore, to develop procedures for identifying conflicts that are likely to arise, as well as systems that can be used to constructively manage these conflicts. In the process, you very likely will discover new opportunities to transform your organization's conflict into a productive learning experience.

Figure 1.3 – Conflicts are predictable and can be anticipated

It is very important that when we deal with conflicts we understand what the issues are. We must also keep in mind that the disagreement we perceive is just that, a perception of our own understandings. We must make sure we understand who is involved in the conflict, if there is a need for us to bring anybody else into the conflict, and how the environment (i.e. the workplace, noise, emotional conditions) is affecting the conflict. We are all motivated people, driven by different goals, and with distinct intensities; these differences in and of themselves are prone to generate conflicts among one another.

We are Motivated People

We are all motivated people. Some of us are more motivated to keep out jobs than others who, believe it or not, tend to be motivated to quit their jobs. Some professionals are motivated to go out of their ways in accomplishing a task while others are motivated to use as little effort as they can. As illustrated in figure 1.4, motivation is an issue of direction and intensity. The variation of such direction and intensity is the cause of most of the conflicts we find ourselves in.

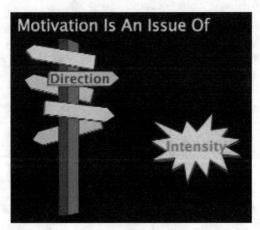

Figure 1.4 – Motivation is an issue of direction and intensity

If we want to fully understand motivation, and how it can trigger conflicts, we have to understand how people select direction and how they choose the amount of intensity they will devote to that direction. At many organizations, people often fail to achieve their targets, their goals. The reason for that is that a person selects the desired target, as illustrated in figure 1.5, such as becoming a senior manager, but has insufficient intensity (i.e. does not invest in developing career and people skills, understanding the organization, volunteering to assist in strategic areas of work, etc.). As a result, although they are working in the right direction, they come up short.

Figure 1.5 – Motivation is an issue of direction and intensity

To succeed the person must have not only the desired direction but also the amount of intensity that is required to hit that target. Sometimes in an organization a person has plenty of intensity but the direction is off, as depicted in figure 1.6. As a result we shoot right past a desired target. Sometimes in organizations a person is pursuing a desired target and doing so with sufficient intensity to reach the target, but another attractive target comes along and pulls that person away from the initial target, as shown in figure 1.7. In that case, despite original good intentions, the person fails to reach the target. In reality, in our lives and our organizations, there are many targets, and those targets are calling for our attention. As a result, for an organization to manage motivation effectively, and therefore conflicts, it has to understand the wide range of targets that is out there, and how people are evaluating each of these targets.

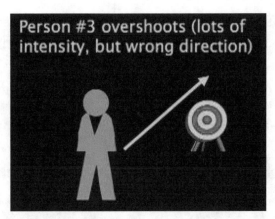

Figure 1.6 – To succeed we must have the desired direction and the right amount of intensity

Figure 1.7 – Multiple targets can reduce the amount of intensity

There are more targets out there than any of us can successfully attain. Motivation is an issue of direction and intensity, and so it is with conflicts. When two or more individuals have different directions, conflict may arise. The higher the intensity of those directions, the more intense will be the level of the conflict. It is our job, and responsibility, to find ways to influence the directions people choose and the amount of intensity that they use as they pursue their targets, thus preventing the conflicts that may arise from these human dynamics.

Dealing with conflicts, therefore, will require a managerial mediation, which is discussed later on in chapter 3. By managerial mediation I mean a dialogue for use by managers, supervisors, team leaders and other counterparts, that involves simple third-party mediation to resolve a conflict between two coworkers for whose performance the manager is responsible. When it comes to mediation, it is very important that you first self-mediate your thoughts in an attempt to acquire a better understanding of the issue at hand. Team mediation also finds its place when dealing with conflict, and we will cover those aspects later on in this book as well. But before attempting to mediate a conflict, one must understand why conflicts occur, and why it is not typical for anyone to attempt to resolve these conflicts naturally.

Chapter 2
Why Do We Avoid Conflict?

Some people hate anything that feels like conflict. They will do almost anything to avoid an argument.[1]

Overview

Most of us hate anything that feels like a conflict. We would do almost anything to avoid an argument, paying it no attention and, hoping the problem will just go away. We end up agreeing to things that we have no intention of doing. We stay in a job long after our enthusiasm for it is dead and gone. When it comes to conflicts, fear tends to take over our behavior and reactions.

In any organization, especially the very dynamic ones, coworkers tend to see conflicts and avoid them, some more than others. But it is not unusual for coworkers to be able to assert themselves competently in one part of the workplace, being self-assertive, able to address issues and readily engage in conflict, and not do so in another . Furthermore, the same people who are so assertive at work may be, in their private lives, a lot different. The opposite is also true; you find people that are very assertive and combative at home with their spouses, but perceived as pacemakers at their organizations, where they are motivated less by gentleness than by fear. Here conflict scares them. In the face of problems they freeze up inside, become passive and may even put off making a decision if they think it will lead to tension. Such attitudes can make a productive team very unproductive, impacting interpersonal relationships within the group. This may also affect the success of a

---

[1] *John R. Ballew*, (2001) Wimping Out, Nelson, NYC.

project, if workers hired for their skills fear expressing opposite opinions about their subject matter expertise.

Rational and logical thinking has been responsible for most achievements in life.   However, as these achievements were archived and access to them became possible, answers to previously unknown problems became searchable, thus limiting and constricting our ability to think creatively, to innovate.   Just think about the automobile industry.   Nothing really has changed, except for the recent forays into hybrid cars, since the invention of automobile. Cars are still running on wheels and burning fossil fuel. Yet following the invention of the wheel, cars pulled by horses, the first steam cars and finally the first engine propelled car, not many years had gone by; nevertheless, each of those stages transcended the next.   The same holds true for the architecture and building construction industries.

I believe, the problem is that we have grown unsecured. Unfortunately, the price of relief from anxiety is the loss of creative ability. This is surely why we lost innovative teachers, who felt there was no room for creativity, with the latest decade of change. At the beginning of the 20th century however, inventors were bold risk-takers, and had to rely a lot on their own instincts, as there was not much memory (libraries, knowledge resources) available other than their own experimentation.

What Bridges a Conflict is a New Conflict

For centuries, the concept of dealing with conflicts didn't exist, as life in and of itself was one big conflict – no wonder the many philosophic schools, in particular the existentialist. However, today's executives, for the most part, are not willing to take risks. After all, many of them are afraid of what the Board will say, how Wall Street will judge them, what will happen if they are wrong, and so on. Instead of bridging gaps with another gap, they get immobilized, becoming victims of their own contradictory impulses.

While delivering a workshop for a group of executives and senior technical managers in Brasilia, BR back in 1988, I talked with at least three executives that clearly wanted to succeed in their business, but at the same time showed all the signals of wanting to fail as well. Everything they did carried both messages. One of them, from a major bank in Brazil, would get very excited about the prospect of automating certain decision-making process within his organization. However, at the same time, all he did all day long was to cripple the project by refusing to delegate, undermining his newly formed taskforce committee, failing to meet deadlines, and stalling on crucial decisions.

Although back then I could not understand the situation -- I too was victim of not wanting to fill my own gaps by just accepting the most plausible excuse – what I realized over and over again throughout the years it that his behavior was not so unusual. Contradictory impulses, which lead to conflicts (and Farson discusses the phenomenon extensively), are present in every project, every team.   Thus every situation, every outcome, every achievement, can be both good and bad. That's why the science of bridging the gaps is essentially a challenge every leader has; the management of dilemmas, of conflicts, and coping with contradictions while appreciating the coexistence of opposites, is crucial to the development of a different way of thinking.

All Things are Impermanent: Bridges Don't Last

It is evident that all things are impermanent, including the bridges used to overcome conflicts. But didn't they use to fade, or change more slowly? Not long ago, businesses were experiencing massive restructurings, re-engineering and redirection; talk about sources for conflict! Skills and tools were needed for response to various impacts, to help us create rather than react. But now we are spinning faster, and the group change tools do not always seem to work. The reason is twofold: mistakenly identifying problems and believing that once a conflict is resolved it will always be resolved.

Both assumptions are incorrect. First, many executives have difficulty distinguishing a conflict from a predicament. Conflicts can always be solved, while predicaments can only be coped with. Spending time and energy on a predicament will only bring frustration, discouragement and desolation. Most issues one faces in life, from marriage, family issues, business affairs and so on are complicated and inescapable dilemmas. They tend to be predicaments that do not makes a single option the best, where all options tend to be relative. Business in the 21st century is a lot like that. By accepting that all things are impermanent, executives can take advantage of business tools that help them solve conflicts and accept predicaments, actually taking advantage of them, as those are very possibly the only consistent data they will have. Thus, some strategies to copy with the paradox of bridging conflicts are discussed throughout this book.

Understanding the Genesis of a Conflict

Imagine for a moment that a conflict is like a tornado. Now, consider the outer limits of this tornado. It is chaotic, as it causes great devastation and change to everything it touches in the organization. Then think of the center of the tornado, the eye. There all is calm, peaceful and quiet. Think of it as your present organizational status. For sure you will not be able to stop or even control the wind and the noise around the organization, be it competition noise, shifting market winds and so on.

While you can maintain yourself at the center of the tornado, and flow with the wind, that is the worst thing you can do. Doing so will only postpone the inevitable, as the periphery of the tornado comes crashing down on your organization. However, this is not a predicament, and therefore has solution. But the solution requires courage and a willingness to fail and die, to crash and burn, as the fishermen did in the movie "A Perfect Storm." But a calculated and well-thought out strategy that transcends the corporate memory and taps into the corporate instinct is hard to come by. Keep in mind that doing little, other than that what seems absolutely safe, could generate much bigger risks than taking a chance. Risks are how we learn from our successes (not mistakes!).

Where Does the Fear of Conflict Come From?

For many people, as illustrated in figure 2.1, the fear of conflict can be traced back to the way they were raised, to their upbringing and cultural background, as discussed in the last chapter. As children, these people may have experienced several arguments and fights between their parents. They may have seen things escalate out of control and end up in abuse or abandonment. If they believe that arguing is going to lead to a loss of friendship, to cause a coworker to become upset or uncooperative, or even lead to fights, it makes sense to avoid the conflict at all costs, even if they need to hide their emotions and opinions. Such behaviors can wrack havoc on any teamwork or business interactions. If workers believe that disagreeing with a supervisor may cost them their job, or that they will be put into the boss's "black book," then the tendency to be passive and avoid a conflict is extremely high, if not predictable.

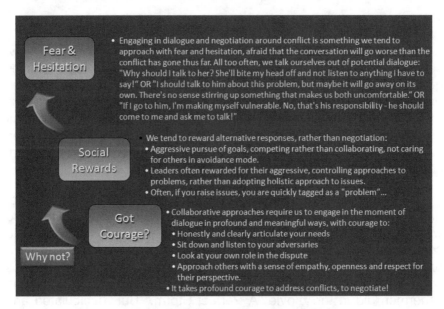

Figure 2.1 – Why we avoid conflicts?

Unfortunately, while most workers should normally engage in conflict at work, as it is inevitable, even with the most perfect coworker prefers to talk about their difference in opinion at the water cooler, turning potentially constructive feedback into gossip. At any professional working environment, misunderstandings will happen from time to time, and a certain amount of conflict is inevitable. It is actually somewhat desirable, as discussed earlier. If in an attempt to avoid a conflict a coworker never argues, always agreeing with the opinions of others, the working relationship is likely to be blunt and superficial, without much innovation, critical thinking or positive synergies.

So why do we avoid conflict? To put it plain and simple, it takes courage to just deal honestly with issues at the workplace, or anywhere for that matter. It takes an effective approach to engage in the moment of dialogue in profound and meaningful ways, with courage to:

- Honestly and clearly articulate needs

- Sit down and listen to adversaries

- Look at your own role in the dispute

- Approach others with a sense of empathy, openness, and respect for their perspective.

In other words, it takes profound courage to address conflicts, to negotiate. "But," you may ask, "why do so many of us not have such courage?" Why not? At the base of it all there are too many factors. The main ones, however, are consequences of social rewards, and fear, or hesitation.

How Social Reward Affects Conflict Avoidance?

Social rewards exercise a major impact in the way we behave and make decisions at the workplace. We tend to reward alternative responses, rather than negotiation. In college, and at the workplace, aggressive personal goals, competition rather than collaboration, and not caring for others by assuming an avoidance approach are all rewarded attitudes. Leaders are often rewarded for their aggressive and controlling approach to problems. They are not motivated to adopt a more holistic approach to conflict. On the contrary, they are driven to adopt a very competitive style of conflict resolution, which often discourages healthy interactions between teams and confrontations that could end up in constructive criticism and new alternatives. Often if you raise issues or concerns that may be part of your expertise, you are quickly tagged as a "problem" employee.

As mentioned earlier, fear and hesitation can also play a major role in conflict resolution. Engaging in dialog and negotiating around conflict is something we tend to approach with fear and hesitation. We tend to be afraid that the conversation will go worse than the conflict has gone thus far. All too often, we talk ourselves out of potential dialogue. We then end up internalizing thoughts and saying things in our minds (or at the water cooler), such as

"Why should I make the effort to talk to him? He will bite my head off and not pay attention to anything I have to say anyway!"

Or

"We should talk to her about this issue, but maybe it will go away on its own, so let's just wait. There is no need to be brewing up a storm that will make us both uncomfortable."

Or

"If I go to her, I am exposing myself and becoming vulnerable before her. No, that is her responsibility; she should come to me and ask me to talk!"

The Cost of Conflicts

As illustrated in Figure 2.2, 42 percent of an employee's time is spent engaging in, or attempting to resolve, a conflict[2]. Conflicts cost money! Much time is wasted talking about them, meeting. mediating, mitigating, and ultimately battling in courts. In the heat of unstructured conflict resolution systems, bad decisions are made, which many times results in the loss of revenue, time, and resources, mainly valuable employees. As a domino-effect, such losses trigger even more unwanted decisions and policies, such as unnecessary restructuring of teams and departments, and low morale and job motivation. These situations often culminate in lost work time, health costs, and at its extreme, sabotage, theft, and general damages to the organization, its projects, image, and workforce.

---

[2] Watson, C. & Roffman, L., "Managers as Negotiators," The Leadership Quarterly 7 (1), 1996, 63-85

- Wasted time
- Bad decisions
- Lost employees
- Unnecessary restructuring
- Sabotage, theft, damage
- Lowered job motivation
- Lost work time
- Health costs

Figure 2.2 – Why we avoid conflicts?

If we take a closer look at the heart of the problem, not only for American business and organizations, but for international and global organizations as well, what we find can be simplified in a very simple equation. As depicted in Figure 2.3, the equation exposes the hidden culprit in the high cost of unresolved conflict: Predictable conflicts plus weak systems equals high costs.

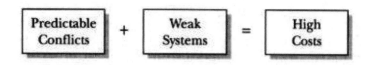

Figure 2.3 – The culprit in high costs of conflict resolution

The following sessions provide a small glimpse on how three leading companies were affected by conflict at their workplace, and

27

the consequences of not having formal training and adequate systems implemented. These are short, mini-cases which illustrate the importance of dealing proactively with conflicts and saving the aggravation along the way. Remember, conflicts are expensive!

Coca-Cola Enterprises

In 1999, Coca-Cola Enterprises found itself in a very difficult situation, as the costs of employee conflict were escalating rapidly and, amidst it all, the company lost a large class action lawsuit brought by its African-American employees. As a response to the problem, Coca-Cola began a series of pilot programs designed to resolve employee disputes within the company rather than wait to settle them in the courts, or through other authoritative agencies. These programs were the beginning of a strategic move toward a different approach to the management of conflict.

Through a consistent and sustained effort, the company committed to invest and develop a "Diversity Council," which then endorsed the development of a conflict management system for Coca-Cola. The system, designed under the leadership of Melanie Lewis, the Manager of Public Management, ultimately developed and implemented what was described as an integrated, comprehensive, and strategic approach to conflict management. The system used an ombudsperson office, mediation and arbitration, training in the use of the system, and a strong set of internal support structures. By 2002, Coca-Cola had put into place a system designed to revolutionize the way it handled employee conflicts and disputes.

PECO Energy

PECO Energy began dealing with the issue of conflict management in a more graphic fashion. Long the most visible nonunion electric utility company in the United States, it faced an International Brotherhood of Electrical Workers (IBEW) organizing campaign in the mid-1990's. While most of the employees did not choose representation in the subsequent election, IBEW representative Robert Speers revealed the employees' conflicts and their unmet needs. Thus, PECO tried to improve conflict resolution within the organization.

That expression of unmet employee needs came through a union organizing campaign was not well accepted by the company's leadership. PECO had put a peer review program for employee disputes in place in 1993, and it had worked well, but senior managers believed not well enough. They felt that opportunities for resolution of conflicts and disputes were being lost. In 1996, they began to evaluate alternatives and additions to the peer review process. Ultimately through benchmarking, internal focus groups, and other data gathering, PECO shuffled to institute a full-blown alternative dispute resolution (ADR) system, including the use of mediation and arbitration.

Schering-Plough

Schering-Plough had a completely different experience. A significant loss in damages, resulting from a sexual harassment case in the mid-1990's, caused the pharmaceutical company's executives to wonder if that case could have been prevented, or the damage minimized, through a more effective conflict resolution system. They assembled a team to consider whether the company should move toward an ADR system of some kind.

Following an extensive benchmarking effort, and a data-based simulation of the potential costs and benefits that might accrue from such a program change, the leaders rejected the adoption of any part of an ADR system. The significant factors in the decision were the speculative nature of the system's supposed benefits and resistance from line management. Therefore, Schering-Plough still struggles to enforce the procedures already in place for the resolution of employee conflicts and disputes with the corporation.

These three cases, Coca-Cola Enterprises, PECO and Schering-Plough, although similar in nature, are not at all alike in the outcomes they produced. When the aches of dispute resolution impact companies in the area of what they consider to be important, their strategies and attitudes differ. Suffice to say that each one of the companies was dissatisfied with the current results and strategies implemented to address employee conflict resolution. Each one of them engaged in a comprehensive analysis of the situation, and each reached a conclusion -- all three different. But each of them was considering a question newly significant to U.S. corporations in the

1990's: is the system in use to manage and resolve conflicts with employees adequately serving our needs?

These three cases are broadly representative of an important trend in organizations: a substantial dissatisfaction with conventional approaches to conflict resolution, and an attempt to improve that satisfaction by replacing old approaches with new, elite-minded conflict resolution systems. The trend of dissatisfaction with current systems, the strategy underlying the current alternatives, and their impact will vary, but the issue remains clear: conflict is expensive. And without a good understanding of the strategies and techniques to resolve such conflict, companies may find themselves in a very hard situation, not only financially, but most of all, in their ability to effectively compete in a marketplace that no longer rewards the biggest organizations, but the most effective ones, the fast ones.

For us at MGCG, based on more than 10 years of practice in the industry, we believe there is something wrong with the way most businesses, governments, schools, and institutions in general manage conflict. In the past two years in particular, we have spent a great deal of time consulting with companies on ways of identifying and resolving conflict. We believe that the failure to understand workers' ability to proactively resolve conflicts lies in a systemic reliance on higher authority (or power play), avoidance, and weak or only partial use of collaborative options.

As figure 2.3 earlier in this chapter shows, there is enough data available today that such a figure is not excusable -- 42 percent of a company's time wasted in dealing with conflict. We have already alluded to three alternative dispute resolutions (ADR) which have demonstrated that, if a business conflict can be resolved through mediation instead of the courts, the parties will save money. And at the same time, they will preserve the possibility of a long-term business relationship instead of ending that relationship. All of these results are achieved without accounting for the fact that as much as 50 to 80 percent in legal fees (in some cases) are saved. Conflict resolution costs money! As discussed in Chapter 1, conflict itself is not the problem, but unresolved conflicts are.

Chapter 3
The Root Cause of Conflict

Conflict is an integral dynamic in the growth and development of living organisms and groups.[1]

Overview

At the professional level, whether deciding to apply for a new job within the company or stay put, go to a graduate school or take a promotion, change departments or roles, conflict is a part of moving through life, from one stage of development to another. This is true in any organization: families, neighborhoods, businesses, government agencies, and multinational corporations.

As discussed earlier in this book, we are all motivated people. The motivation of the parties involved in a conflict is clearly at the heart of any conflict situation. If a conflict is to be avoided or stopped, this motivation must be understood, and the conditions leading to a predisposition to conflict reduced or eliminated. This chapter aims to sketch out the elements that determine such motivation. While the focus is on economic motivation, other factors (political, cultural) are also obviously of importance. Such factors -- themselves influenced and sometimes determined by economic factors -- decide the way people view themselves, and are viewed (i.e. the groups they form). They play a large role in the distribution of resources and are a key factor in any conflict resolution strategy. In fact, it is rarely possible to disentangle political, cultural and economic elements from conflicts, as each is embedded in the other.

---

[1] Karl A. Slaikeu, Ralph H. Hasson (2002) *Controlling the Cost of Conflicts*, *Jossey-Bass.*

For technical professionals it is no different. The Marketing Department, for instance, tells the production line that they need the product by a particular date, and that cost cannot exceed a certain price. The design engineer is quick to emphasize that this cannot be done. After all, his main concern is for the quality of the product. The main issue here is not whether the Marketing Department and the Production Department see things the same way (they never will), but rather how will we resolve the conflict that the differences between them evinces, while delivering a high-quality product that meets the customer's needs, on time, which should lead to more business for the company in the future.

If the Marketing and Production Departments are capable of handling the conflict well, this can be a creative opportunity for improvement in relationships and organizational productivity. If they are able to overcome this interdepartmental conflict, the design engineers and the marketing group, they could develop new strategies to work together, and may create a new method for problem solving. These departments may even develop a new strategy whereby they could work together from the initiation phase of a project, developing specification and sale strategies for the new product. If these departments succeed in solving their conflict, and therefore their differences, they may emerge more confident about their relationship to one another and their ability to work together, despite the differences. Such an approach will take what is known as "conflict transformation."

As discussed in Chapter 2, conflicts occur when the ideas, interests, or behaviors of two or more individuals or groups clash. The clash can be a minor exchange of words, or it can take the form of behind-the-scenes jockeying for position -- deciding to change dramatically a project or kill it while the main proponent is on vacation or a business trip. As we will see in this chapter, such conflicts may lead to power plays, as I once saw a disgruntled employee after a layoff continue to show up at the company every day to have lunch with other employees, and to talk about what had happened to her, influencing employees to quit the company.

To clarify, throughout this book the type of conflict with which I am concerned is organized group conflict: that is to say, conflicts that are not exclusively a matter of individuals randomly breaking rules, having differences of opinion or, worse, committing violence against others. What is involved is group mobilization, as many technical professionals work in teams – many in virtual teams --, and need to understand the underlying motivation for such mobilization. By teams I mean a group of professionals who identify with each other, for certain purposes, as against those outside the group, normally also identifying some other group with whom they are in conflict. Group organization may be quite informal, but it exists, implying that there is some agreement, implicit or not, on purposes and activities within the group.

This means that normally there are those within any group instigating conflict who lead or orchestrate the conflict, including constructing or enhancing the perception of group identity in order to achieve group mobilization. There are also those who actively carry out the fighting, or give it some support - for short, we shall call these two leaders and followers, though there can be considerable overlap between the two categories. The conflict is not, at least purportedly, the objective; rather it is instrumental, used in order to achieve other ends. Usually, the declared objective is political -- to secure or sustain power within the organization or group -- while power is wanted for the advantages it offers. However, political motivation may disappear or become less important, and the conflict is then pursued for the economic advantage (i.e. promotions, personal gains, innovation projects, etc.) conferred directly on those involved. But even then conflicts remain predominantly group activities.

Conflict can have many causes, as depicted in Figure 3.1. Typically it results from compound interest, poor communication, maybe even intent on the part of one party, or selfishness. Conflicts can also be caused by personality disorders, or scarce resources. But as discussed in Chapters 1 and 2, conflict, at the root, is always a threat to personal needs, or caused by fear. Conflict can also occur at a high level of the organization, among partners and shareholders, when, for example, there is discussion on two organizations joining forces to compete for its work. In addition, certain factors at work may exist that worsen issues and generate conflicts (i.e. work environment, favoritism, politics, etc...).

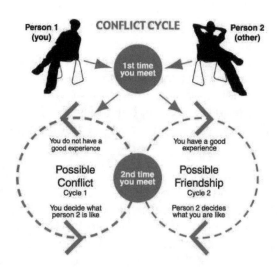

Figure 3.1 – Conflict cycle: going through the causes

Most often, conflicts are associated with three sets of parties in any organization: employees, customers and clients, and partners, which include shareholders, owners, and stakeholders. The employees, or workers, are those that take a paycheck, whether hourly workers, or board members. There are predictable conflicts within this group, which involve supervision, definition of team goals, project planning, project execution, allocation of resources, interpersonal relationships, communication, and violation of legally protected rights, such as sexual harassment and age or racial discrimination.

Customers and clients are those parties who buy products and services, and can also be a source of conflict for any organization. For instance, a customer or client buys a training program and finds, a month after the training has been delivered, that the primary goals are not achieved. The resulting complaint puts the customer in conflict with the service provider. Unless conflict resolution systems, as discussed in Chapter 2, are implemented and shared with the stakeholders, in this case the customer, conflicts are prone to arise. For instance, at MGCG, whenever we are in the process of negotiating a training program, part of the discussion includes an understanding of the *keys for success*. The goal is to make sure that all parts involved in the project – the business unit, the training professionals, the client, and the trainees -- are aware of the goals and objectives of the program, that every constituent will be able to assess if the program has be successful or not, and what are the next steps. In our case, we use evaluation forms to assess the quality of the instructor and the course materials, as well as what the expectations were on the part of the trainees.

Know What Matters

Michael Korda, the novelist, once said that "the first rule of success, and the one that supersedes all others, is to have energy. It is important to know how to concentrate it and focus it on the important things, instead of frittering it away on trivia.[2]" The most powerful thing you can do at any moment is re-focus. Ask yourself: What do you want to achieve? Why is this important?

Keep in mind that conflicts (or what I call gaps) are inevitable, and you will always have to deal with the consequences of change in the organization. And the fact your organization is learning (it should be) only makes the advent of change even more obvious, as awareness is part of the process. Once you learn that there is no face lost in abandoning all hope of completely avoiding conflict, you can much more comfortably get down to the task of managing conflict, deciding which bits of it are worthy of your attention and, more importantly, which are not.

Your goal should always be of bridging the gap, which is the same as transcending, not adapting. Many people come to this epiphany when they have their second child. All the angst spent worrying about potential crises with the first child turns into considered risk management. With the first one it's "Oh my Gosh - keep him away from that - it's got dirt on it!!," and panic sets in. With the second one it's "Well, it's only dirt," and serenity flows. With conflict it is similar. Once you learn that conflicts are part of business and transcending them is part of the thrill, you then become a knowing organization, dependent on the next conflict, so you can learn one more time and set distance from your competitors. Much like surfers, you should look at conflicts as waves, the necessary element for a fun ride, full of emotions, accomplishments and lessons learned.

---

[2] *Another Life: A Memoir of Other People*, Delta, 2000.

The trick is to continually assess issues based on the amount of influence you have in determining the outcomes of conflict. If you have no influence, your worrying isn't going to help, so don't worry. If you have a moderate amount, do what you can and be satisfied that you've done your best. If you have great influence, then set it as a priority and influence away. No time to worry.

Root Causes of Conflicts

There are many causes for conflict, and to be successful in resolving them you must identify the areas in which you and the other party agree. In other words, as depicted in Figure 3.2, what is the last point of agreement? From there you can then work out a way where the parties are willing to make concessions or accommodate each other to the benefit of the project, or the whole. Much more will be discussed on this issue in later chapters.

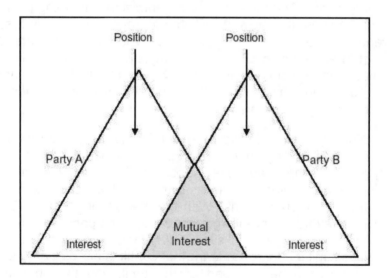

Figure 3.2 – Finding a point of mutual interest as a strategy to resolve conflicts.

What are the root causes of conflict? In my experience we always find one or more of the following in every complaint, conflict, or full-blown dispute involving individuals and groups at organizations:

- **Denial** -- some people will not accept that they are in the middle of a conflict, or they will not see it, even if someone is screaming in their ear. A plant manager at a power generation company told me once that he did not see that there was a problem with his group until it was too late. He only realized it when he got a resignation letter from one of his key employees, and another one requesting to transfer to another department.

- **Lack of skills** -- many of the conflicts in a work team or a project typically happen because of the lack of skills that the team members or the employees possess. All too often employees are poor communicators, negotiators, project managers and leaders. In addition, upper management tends not to give much emphasis on conflict resolution training. Furthermore, some employees are more trainable than others. Also, this type of training is best when delivered in-house, in-company, using real issues on hand. Training at public facilities, such as hotels, leaves out a major component of conflict and its resolution: the work environment, including peers, project nuances and the management team.

- **Lack of information** – Too often, for lack of project management skills, organizations don't have a communication plan in place. As a result, project teams are often misinformed, or do not have enough information about a process, a product, a service, or a procedure. Conflicts often arise when those less privileged, that may not have access to information such as direct reports, come in contact with upper management. The opposite can also be true, where upper management is not aware of the day-to-day operations of a group, and end up making poor decisions and impacting the entire group or product. Communication is the key to managing conflict, solving problems and producing the desired outcome of any interaction.

- **Conflicting interests** – In chapters 1 and 2 we discussed the fact that everyone in a organization has distinct targets and intensities in achieving those targets. As if that was not enough, every employee also has distinct sets of values, views about right and wrong, good and bad, as well as their own priorities. In addition, some are more prone to take risks, while others are risk-averted.

- **Psychopathology** – According to research, about 10 to 20 percent of the workforce has suffered or suffers some type of psychopathology, such as acute stress, clinical depression, or character disorder. Some professionals are aware of their condition, some take medications, and others have no idea of it, or are in denial. Other professionals may be addicted to alcohol, drugs or other substances. All these aspects are prone to create conflict with coworkers and team members.

- **Personality** – Some personalities are not meant to work together and end up clashing. In the next chapter we will discuss conflict resolution styles, and how they impact the ability of workers to interact, be effective as a team and deal with conflict. But for now, suffice to say that some people, typically known as troublemakers, are always looking for a reason to disagree, while others, conflict avoiders, are always looking for ways out of a potential conflict. Some people are more aggressive, while others are more understanding. These differences in personality will also impact the level of conflict and the ability to resolve it.

- **Lack of resources** – This is one of the major generators of conflict at organization, especially around deadlines. As staff is reduced, either by downsizing or rightsizing, the pressure to keep productivity up is increased. So is stress, which will find its way out through poor communication – or lack of it -- and clash of personalities, if not absenteeism.

- **Organizational deficiencies** – The lack of policies and procedures at the organization can be a major catalyst for conflict. For instance, the lack of an employee handbook outlining the dos and don'ts of the organization can be the cause of unnecessary conflict. Also, if the organization does not have a system of communication and project management, the information chain, if it exists at all, will easily be broken, generating, therefore, more conflict.

- **Selfishness** – This is one of the greatest causes of conflict. If you are taking more of your share, someone will definitely point it out and complain; it doesn't matter if the issue is money, time off, office space, work breakdown structure, and so on.

- **Sabotage** – This is the level of conflict that escapes, very often, explanation.

Conflict Transformation

Conflicts happen for a reason. Attempting to resolve the conflict does not mean that we necessarily need to give up on the reason for it. In other words, the resolution of the conflict should not be another way to cover up changes that are really necessary. Conflicts are normal in any organization and work relationship, and conflict is necessary for change to happen. While there are some debates on the term of *conflict resolution* versus *conflict transformation*, in my view, conflict transformation is a stage in the conflict resolution process. As illustrated in Figure 3.3, once there is an understanding of the conflict and its roots, all parties involved in the conflict must engage in a constructive change effort that includes, and goes beyond, the resolution of the specific problems.

Figure 3.3 shows that for a conflict transformation to take place, all parties involved in the conflict must go through the three inquiry stages:

- **Inquiry 1** - the first stage, *presenting situation*, calls for understanding of the issue at three levels. The broader level, which encompasses the history of the issue, the conflict; the mid-level, which determines all the issues in conflict; and at the core of the issue, or center, the person's interests, needs, and fears.

- **Inquiry 2** - the second level focuses on the *horizon of future*. It also calls for understanding of the issue at three levels: the broader level deals with the system used to resolve conflict (if any is in place); the mid-level deals with the relationships at play, where power plays, politics, and corporate policies play a major role; and at the core of the issue lies the potential solutions for the conflict.

- **Inquiry 3** - the third level is focused on the *development of change processes*. This level is the result of inquiry 1 and 2 coming into play. It takes into consideration the personal relations, known cultural and structural aspects of the conflict. At the core of the resolution or the transformation lies the episode of the conflict and the center that generates the conflict. If mediated well (self-mediation or team-mediation), at this level transformation should be promoted.

The Big Picture of Conflict Transformation

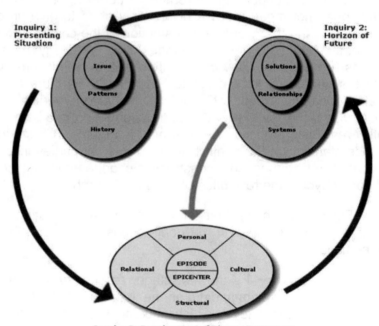

Inquiry 1: Presenting Situation

Inquiry 2: Horizon of Future

Issue
Patterns
History

Solutions
Relationships
Systems

Personal
Relational
EPISODE
EPICENTER
Cultural
Structural

Inquiry 3: Development of Change Processes

Figure 3.3 – Conflict transformation process

If you are going to attempt to resolve a conflict, the process can be simple or complex. It can take one or many meetings, while other conflicts may take an ongoing process and, in some cases, the use of outside mediators. Creativity, as we will discuss in more detail in the chapters to come, will be very important in resolving conflict. Being creative at times just means taking a look at the conflict from a different perspective. Taking a creative approach to conflict management often results in simplifying the problem so that the solution becomes obvious. Whatever approach is taken, if it is well thought out, it will at least begin to move the situation toward resolution.

A Matter of Communication: Avoiding Predicaments

Richard Farson, in his book *Whoever Makes the Most Mistakes Wins*[3] encourages leaders to think "beyond the conventional wisdom...to understand how the ways we think shape what we see, and how paradox and absurdity inevitably play a part in our every action." According to him, we think we want creativity or change, but we really don't, because it requires conflict, and of course, we run from it! We therefore stifle creativity by playing intellectual games, judging and evaluating, dealing in absolutes, thinking stereotypically, and not trusting our own experiences (and training our employees not to trust theirs), as if we instinctively know that by doing so would drag us into a conflict, with ourselves or others, if not both.

Nonetheless, although it is true that leadership is trapped by many paradoxes, communication can be an important vehicle to bridge and manage conflict. Communication provides the link through which information is shared, opinions are expressed, feedback is provided and goals are formulated. Conflicts cannot be resolved without communication. It is necessary to communicate in order to advise, train and inform. Members of an organization must translate corporate goals into action and results. In order for this to happen, all forms of correspondence must flow freely throughout the organizational structure.

There is also a correlation between the willingness of every level of the organization to communicate openly and frequently, and the satisfaction expressed by the workers. Most organizational predicaments, from misunderstandings to disasters, from small frustrations to major morale problems, can be traced back to either a lack of communication or ineffective technique.

---

[3] Free Press, 2002

Communication does not take place unless there is understanding between the communicator and the audience. Simply learning to write or read or speak is not enough. Does one make music by merely striking the keys of a piano? The difference between making noise and making music is study, understanding technique, and practice, practice, practice. The same is true for communication. The difference between talking, reading, writing or hearing, and communicating, is study, understanding technique, and practice, practice, practice.

Therefore, executive staff should examine the process of communication within the organization and strive to increase their propensity for successful communication. Messages must be clearly stated, brief and well-planned, and must answer the questions who, what, when, where and why.

The sending modes of communication are speaking, writing and nonverbal messages. The receiving modes are listening, reading and observation. Each of these modes are used in the process of getting work accomplished. Improvement in the effectiveness of any one of these modes will result in higher productivity and increased satisfaction. It is not simply a matter of how much one communicates, but how well.

Bridging the Gap From the Top Dow or From the Bottom Up?

Organizational leaders are perpetually faced with a series of questions:

- In bridging a major gap or conflict (a change effort), should they drive the change, or build the bridge, from the top down, or must it have bottom up leadership?

- How would you make sure your organization is constantly innovating, and at the same time delivering a standardized level of service with a certain level of fostered conflict?

- How would you encourage your senior management group to work as a team and at the same time not lose your star performers as conflict inevitably arises?

As discussed earlier in this chapter, what these three questions all have in common is that they cannot be answered using solely logical methods. Yet, one of the bedrock principles of science is the universal applicability of logic. But an understanding and a facility with paradoxes is as important, if not more important, than understanding logic.

Although leadership is defined above as the management of paradoxes, paradoxes are not managed in the way that problems are. Paradoxes have to be constantly managed, for they are never "solved" like problems. Additionally, a paradox can be a critical concept to integrity. If a concept is paradoxical, that in itself should suggest that it smacks of integrity, which gives off the ring of truth. Conversely, if a concept is not in the least paradoxical, you should be suspicious of it and suspect that it has failed to integrate some aspect of the whole. Such a premise is very important in generating and evaluating Thomas Koulopoulos'[4] concept of collective corporate wisdom.

It is common today for CEOs to report that all management is people management. Given that Christianity, also, could be described as being about people management, it is not surprising that the work world and the religious world would share the phenomenon of paradox. It would help, therefore, if there was a path in and out of conflict. Well, there is, even though it may not be exactly what you are looking for.

---

[4] Koulopoulos et al. (1997), *Corporate Instinct: Building a Knowing Enterprise for the 21st Century*, Wiley.

Chapter 4
The Path Through and Out of a Conflict

There is only one truth, steadfast, healing, salutary, and that is the absurd.[1]

Overview

A framework for understanding conflict is an organizing strategy that brings such events into better focus. There are several ways these strategies can be used, and each of us will find some more amenable to our own ways of thinking than others. So, what works for some of us may not work for others. Moreover, the strategies presented in this chapter are not equally applicable to all conflicts. Seldom would we apply all of them at the same time to the same situation. Nevertheless, together they provide a set of concepts that can help us understand the nature of conflict and the dynamics of how conflict unfolds and can be resolved.

Every organization, every department, every team, creates a culture of conflict, a complex set of words, ideas, values, behaviors, attitudes, archetypes, customs, and rules that strongly influence how its members think about and respond to conflict. A corporate culture of conflict is shaped in and by the experiences of its employees and leaders. The employees accept parameters for what they believe is possible when they are in conflict and define what they can reasonably expect, both of themselves and others. The truth of the matter is, in the words of Rainer Maria Rilke[2],

---

[1] Andrew Salmon (2005) *Marswalk One: First Steps on a New Planet,* Springer.
[2] *The Selected Poetry of Rainer Maria Rilke,* (1989), Vintage.

Only someone who is ready for everything, who does not exclude any experience, even the most incomprehensible, will live the relationship with another person as something alive and will himself sound the depths of his own being. For if we imagine this individual as a larger or smaller room, it is obvious that most people come to know only one corner of the room, one spot near the window, one narrow strip on which they keep walking back and forth. And yet how much more human is the dangerous insecurity that drives those prisoners in Poe's stories to feel out the shapes of their horrible dungeons, and not be strangers to the unspeakable terror of the cells. We, however, are not prisoners.

Rilke's passage tells us a lot about how we deal with undesired situations such as conflicts. Since we are not prisoners, however, we tend to shape our capacity to ask questions, alter how we see the people we have conflicts with, and ourselves, and tell us what is acceptable and what is not. The truth of the matter is that we are free to decide how we will deal with a conflict at any given moment. Every organization generates spoken and unspoken rules about what we should and should not say, and do, when we are in a conflict. We all have our conflict styles –subject of this chapter--, regardless if we are aware of them are not. Each of the styles and entities produce a separate and distinct culture that exerts enormous pressure on us to respond to conflict in traditionally expected ways.

Many organizational cultures place a premium on conflict avoidance, as discussed in Chapter 2, whereas others reward other conflict resolution styles, such as accommodating/avoiding or compromising. A number of highly competitive corporate cultures give high marks for aggressive or competing styles. Most organizations have a subtle set of rules regarding who can behave how, with whom, and over what. Figure 4.1 lists the key attributes of the main conflict resolution style.

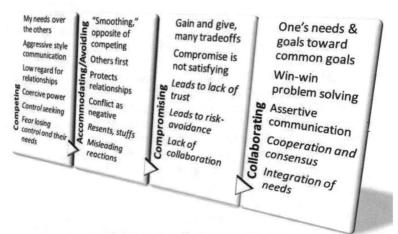

Competing	Accommodating/Avoiding	Compromising	Collaborating
My needs over the others	"Smoothing," opposite of competing	Gain and give, many tradeoffs	One's needs & goals toward common goals
Aggressive style communication	Others first	Compromise is not satisfying	Win-win problem solving
Low regard for relationships	Protects relationships	Leads to lack of trust	Assertive communication
Coercive power	Conflict as negative	Leads to risk-avoidance	Cooperation and consensus
Control seeking	Resents, stuffs	Lack of collaboration	Integration of needs
Fear losing control and their needs	Misleading reactions		

Try to understand conflicts by examining the consequences of behaviors. Watch for conflict styles in achieving one's goals.

Figure 4.1 – Main conflict resolution styles and their attributes

Is Conflict a Perception?

As discussed earlier, a conflict is the result of a series of beliefs that your own needs, interests, wants, or values are incompatible with someone else's, or in danger, threatened. There are both objective and subjective elements to this cognitive dimension. As a practical matter, you may find it useful to think of a conflict as existing if at least one person believes it to exist. If I believe us to have incompatible interests, and act accordingly, then I am engaging you in a conflict process, whether you share this perception or not.

But a conflict is also a feeling, and involves an emotional reaction to situations or interactions that signal a disagreement of some kind. Some of the emotions we may feel, as addressed earlier in this book, may range from fear and sadness to bitterness, anger, or hopelessness. If we experience these feelings in regard to another person or situation, we feel that we are in conflict - and therefore we are. In my professional practice I have see people act as if they were in deep trouble, deep conflict, but not able to figure out the cause of the conflict. They were not sure either, but they sure felt uneasy about the situation, knowing something was not right. Often a conflict exists because at least one person feels in conflict with the other, even though they may not feel the same about it. The behavioral component may be minimal, but the conflict is still very real to the person experiencing the feelings.

Is Conflict an Action?

Yes, conflicts do consist of actions taken by us to express our feelings, convey our perceptions and needs in a way that has the potential of affecting someone else's ability to get his or her own needs met. Often, this can turn into an exercise of power, and turn violent, destructive. By the same token, such actions may be conciliatory, constructive and friendly. No matter the tone, however, the purpose of a conflict action is either to express the conflict or to get one's needs met.

The potential for conflict often exist among people or organizations that interact with each other. Unless people want to think of themselves as constantly in conflict with everyone in their lives, it is more useful to view conflict as existing only when it clearly manifests itself along one of the three dimensions.

Although there are some significant dangers to attributing personal characteristics or motivational structures to systems, practically speaking, I think systems in conflict often experience that conflict on all three dimensions. Although we might better use terms like culture, ethos, public opinion, or popular beliefs to signify the greater complexity and different nature of these dimensions in social systems, conflict among groups clearly has cognitive and affective dimensions, as well as a behavioral dimension.

Conflict Resolution Styles

As we have already established, people respond to conflict in many different ways, starting with avoidance and escalating beyond negotiation to a less desirable, and at times costly, destructive approach. Many people draw on interpersonal skills to respond to situations in which one person's interests collide with the interests of another.

At the interpersonal skill level, a conflict can be handled fairly and nonviolently by the parties with conflicting interests. If negotiations are attempted and they go well, there is no reason for any other conflict response. But we know that many conflicts escalate to other, less desirable forms. Moreover, if you attempt, as you read this chapter, to identify your current organizational culture, you very likely will search in vain for signs of meaningful support for genuine collaboration with those you have conflicts with: creative dialogues regarding problems, honest and empathetic self-critical leadership in addressing and respond to conflicts, and a preventative, persistent, and systemic approach to conflict resolution.

Instead, what you probably will find are dismissive attitudes that regard conflict resolution as pointless or *touchy-feely*. Also very typical are conflict-averse cultures, ones that reward avoidance and accommodation attitudes, or aggressive and hypercompetitive cultures, ones that permit retribution and reprisal for speaking the truth. Last but not least, you will also find bureaucratic rules that encourage passive-aggressive behavior, hypocritical and self-serving leadership, and covert systems that create chronic and avoidable conflicts.

Unfortunately, in most organizational cultures, it is rare that aggression, avoidance, and accommodation require explanation, whereas collaboration, honesty, openness, and forgiveness tend are seldom acceptable. Albert Camus comes to mind; when observing similar phenomenon, he wrote that "Through a curious transposition peculiar to our times, it is innocence that is called upon to justify itself[3]."

The Competing Style

The person with a competing style advocates his own needs over the needs of others. This style relies on aggressive communication, low regard for future relationships, and the exercise of coercive power. Those using a competitive style tend to seek control over a discussion, in both substance and ground rules. They fear that loss of such control will result in solutions that fail to meet their needs. Competing tends to result in responses that increase the level of threat.

The overuse of this style can lead to a lack of feedback, reduced learning, and low empowerment, which can result in being surrounded by "yes-men" (or -women). People who abuse of this style often use inflammatory words and statements, due to a lack of interpersonal skills training. In extreme cases, the person may create

---

[3] The Plague, 1947.

errors in the implementation of the task by withholding needed information, talking behind another person's back (or "backstabbing"), using eye motions and gestures designed to express disapproval, and creating distractions by fiddling or interrupting. Overuse of this style can be exhibited through constant tension or anger and occasional outbursts of violent temper.

The under use of the competing style, however, leads to a lowered level of influence, indecisiveness, slow action, and withheld contributions. People that under use this style tend to justifying their behaviors, demand concessions as a condition of working on the issue, and threaten the breakup of the group or team, as a way of making others give in. Such people also tend to launch personal attacks.

The Accommodating Style

The accommodating style, also categorized as *smoothing*, is the opposite of competing. Persons using this style yield their needs to those of others, trying to be diplomatic. They tend to allow the needs of the group to overwhelm their own, which may never be stated, as preserving the relationship is seen as most important. This style is low in assertiveness and high in cooperativeness, where the goal is to yield. The accommodating style is very appropriate in situations when you need to demonstrate that you are reasonable, foster performance in workgroups, develop good will, maintain peace, have a need to retreat, or for issues of low importance. This style also includes the ability to sacrifice one's own interest, to be selfless, to abide orders, and to yield.

The overuse of the accommodating style can result in ideas getting little attention, restricted influence, loss of contribution, and anarchy. People who overuse this style exhibit a lack of desire to change and usually demonstrate anxiety over future uncertainties. Therefore, their main desire may often be to keep everything the same. The overuse of this style can also exhibit behaviors where the individual tends to give up personal space, making "poor me" or other victim statements, being overly helpful and then holding a grudge, and speaking in an extremely quiet, almost unintelligible voice.

The under use of the accommodating style can result in lack of interaction with other peers and, consequently, rapport. It can also develop low morale and an inability to yield. The under use of the accommodating style may cause a person to display apathy as a way of not addressing anger or hurt, and to make statements full of innuendo and double meaning.

The Avoiding Style

The avoiding style is a very common response to the negative perception of conflict. "Perhaps if we don't bring it up, it will blow over," we say to ourselves. Generally, though, all that happens is that feelings are pent up, views go unexpressed, and the conflict festers until it becomes too big to ignore. Like a cancer that may well have been cured if treated early, the conflict grows and spreads until it kills the relationship. Because needs and concerns go unexpressed, people are often confused, wondering what happened. In an avoiding style, your concerns, or the concerns of the counterpart in the conflict is never satisfied. There is very low level (if not a lack!) of assertiveness and cooperativeness in this style. The goal is always to delay.

It is appropriate, however, to use this style when there are issues of low importance, or to reduce tensions, or even to buy time. The avoiding style can also be appropriate when you are in a low power position and have little control over the situation. This is a situation when you don't have enough influence or power, and need to allow others to deal with the conflict, or when the problem is symptomatic of a much larger issue, that will take some time before you can get to the core of it. When using this style, it is very important that you use foresight in knowing when to withdraw, learn to sidestep loaded questions or sensitive areas by using diplomacy, and become skillful at creating a sense of timing, tending to leave things unresolved.

The overuse of the avoidance style may result in a low level of input, decision-making by default, and allowing issues to fester, which can jeopardize the communication between team members. The avoidance style, or conflict avoiders, can also inhibit brainstorming sessions from being productive and prevent teams from performing effectively. Conflict avoiders tend to feel they cannot speak frankly without fear of repercussions. Typically, conflict avoiders are the result of childhood experiences, past work-related incidents, and negative experiences with conflict resolution. People that tend to be conflict avoiders tend to be silent at meetings or when they should be speaking up, angry, and can be less than truthful when asked if something is wrong. Procrastination is actually a mild form of conflict avoidance. As well as those individual that inappropriately and deliberately takes an opposing point of view during a decision-making situation. Timidity and shyness is another characteristic of a conflict avoider.

When a person is extremely conflict avoiding, behaviors that may follow include negativism, critical and sarcastic comments, or becoming passive aggressive (by being late to meetings, work, or appointments, and not paying attention at meetings). By the same token, the under use of this style may results in hostility and hurt feelings, work can become overwhelming because too many issues are taken on at once, which for a conflict avoider may result in an inability to prioritize and delegate.

The Compromising Style

The compromising style is an approach to conflict in which you gain and give in a series of tradeoffs. While as a style this may be minimally satisfactory, compromise is typically not entirely satisfying, as we tend to remain shaped by our own perceptions of our needs and typically do not understand the interests of others very well. As a result, we may retain a lack of trust and avoid the risk-taking that is involved in more collaborative behaviors. This style is always attempting to find a middle ground, giving and asking for concessions. This is a fairly assertive and cooperative style, with a goal to reach mutual agreements.

The compromising style can be effective when used with issues of moderate importance, where both parties are equally powerful and equally committed to opposing views. This style tends to produce temporary resolution to conflicts, which is appropriate when time is a concern, or as an exit strategy if competing or collaborating styles fail. Compromising skills include the ability to communicate and keep the dialogue open, the ability to find an answer that is fair to both parties, the ability to give up part of what you want, and the ability to assign value to all aspects of the issue.

If overly emphasized, the compromising style can lead to loss of long-term goals, a lack of trust, creation of a cynical environment, and being viewed as having no firm values. Overuse of compromise can result in making concessions to keep people happy without resolving the original conflict. If underused, this style may lead to unnecessary confrontations, frequent power struggles, and ineffective negotiating.

The Collaborating Style

The collaborating style is the pooling of individual needs and goals toward a common goal. Collaboration requires assertive communication and cooperation in order to achieve a better solution than either individual could have achieved alone. It offers the chance for consensus and brings new time, energy, and ideas to resolve the dispute meaningfully. This style's main concern is to satisfy both sides. It is highly assertive and highly cooperative, with the goal to find a "win/win" solution.

The appropriate use of collaborating style may include integrating solutions, learning environments, and the merging of perspectives to gain commitment and to improve relationships. Using this style can also support open discussion of issues, task proficiency, and the equal distribution of work amongst team members. It can foster improved brainstorming sessions, and development of creative problem solving. This style is very appropriate in a team and team-building environment. Collaborating skills include the ability to use active or effective listening, to confront situations in a non-threatening way, and to analyze input and identify underlying concerns.

The overuse of the collaborating style, however, can lead to spending too much time on trivial matters, a diffusion of responsibility, and being overloaded with work. Under use can result in quick-fix solutions, lack of commitment by other team members, disempowerment, and loss of innovation.

Effective Leadership Does Not Avoid Conflicts

I believe that most executives may not have a problem with this, but as Wall Street gets more and more sensitive about the financial perception of an organization, there are executives that waste an enormous amount of time and energy in developing and maintaining a peachy mask and avoiding conflicts. Today's business environment allows no time for that! It's time for empowerment.

Some areas you should be aware of include:

- Protecting the organization's interests from unscrupulous profit-making schemes

- Protecting organizations from unscrupulous tax shelter schemes

- Addressing privacy issues generated by the Internet and other new technologies

- Monitoring the stewardship of the organization's assets

A Matter of Communication: Avoiding Predicaments

Richard Farson[4] encourages leaders to think "beyond the conventional wisdom...to understand how the ways we think shape what we see, and how paradox and absurdity inevitably play a part in our every action." According to him, we think we want creativity or change, but we really don't. We stifle creativity by playing intellectual games, judging and evaluating, dealing in absolutes, thinking stereotypically, and not trusting our own experiences (and training our employees not to trust theirs).

Nonetheless, although it is true that leadership is trapped by many paradoxes, communication can be an important vehicle to bridge conflicts at organizations. Communications provide the link through which information is shared, opinions are expressed, feedback is provided and goals are formulated. Conflicts cannot be resolved without great communication. It is necessary to communicate in order to advise, train and inform. Members of an organization must translate corporate goals into action and results. In order for this to happen, all forms of correspondence must flow freely throughout the organizational structure.

There is also a correlation between the willingness of every level of the organization to communicate openly and frequently, and the satisfaction expressed by the workers. Most organizational predicaments from misunderstandings to disasters; from small frustrations to major morale problems can be traced back to either a lack of communication or to ineffective technique. Communication does not take place unless there is understanding between the communicator and the audience. Simply learning to write or read or speak is not enough. Does one make music by merely striking the keys of a piano? The

---

[4] In *Managing of the Absurd: Paradox in Leadership* (1997), Touchstone Books.

difference between making noise and making music requires study, understanding technique and practice, practice, practice. The same is true for communications. The difference between talking, reading, writing or hearing and communicating is study, understanding technique and practice, practice, practice.

Moving Forward: Overcoming Conflicts

Our challenge is to ease ourselves from these pointless, unproductive cultural patterns and create organizational conflict resolution cultures that value openness, honesty, dialogue, collaborative negotiation, conflict resolution, and the ability to learn from those who we have conflicts with. One of the most important aspects of avoiding conflicts and being able to deal with conflicts proactively is my handling your own emotions.

Managing Your Own Emotions

If you find yourself in a potential conflict, make sure to keep at all cost the following three premises:

- Don't indulge yourself or others in a conflict!

- Don't deny openness, alternatives, creativity, and most importantly, second chances!

- If you are going to be in a conflict, make sure to create richer relationships in the process!

When you begin to realize you are in a conflict your emotions will be the ones giving you the signals, through being angry, hurt, or frightened. We are all capable of improving the way we respond to conflict, and as we do so, we also should gradually begin to change the conflict resolution cultures we have created or tolerated around us. We can, for instance, reduce the level of conflict avoidance simply by honestly and non-aggressively communicating our differences and openly discussing our issues with others in the spirit of trying to find better solutions.

When dealing with conflict in teams, as well among smaller groups, we should adopt a series of synergetic attitudes to solve and avoid future conflicts. We can:

- Empathize with our opponents and acknowledge their contributions to our learning and improvements we have made

- Discuss disagreements publicly and not allow them to be swept under the rug

- Be self-critical about the rule we have played in a conflicts

- Agree not to engage in a caustic insults and vitriolic e-mail attacks on others

- Encourage our colleagues to let go of ancient, unresolved grievances and create common ground with each other

- Encourage consensus regarding vision, mission, goals, and shared values

- Publicly identify covert passive-aggressive behaviors and unethical leadership behaviors, and ask people whether they want to engage in them

- Encourage our team-workers and coworkers to honestly and empathetically communicate deep thoughts and feelings about how they are interacting, and ask them how they would prefer to interact in the future

- Invite our adversaries, those we have conflicts with, to engage in dialogue and collaborative negotiation to solve the problems

- Reach forgiveness and reconciliation within ourselves, and let others know how and why we did so.

By embracing these attitudes and activities, we can start to reorient the conflict-averse and avoidant, as well as the aggressive elements in an organizational culture. More importantly, we can increase everyone's awareness of the subtle forms of violence and prejudice we routinely practice against each other and choose to be both committed and collaborative when we are in conflict.

The contrast between these opposing cultural attitudes can be found, for instance, in the metaphors and language people use when they are in conflict. When such attitudes persist, conflict mediation might be in order, as the parties in conflict would have taken an emotional path to conflict resolution, as opposed to a more cognitive one described above. Figure 4.2 illustrates such a path and the consequences it brings. The focus of Chapter 5 is precisely on understanding mediation and how to mediate.

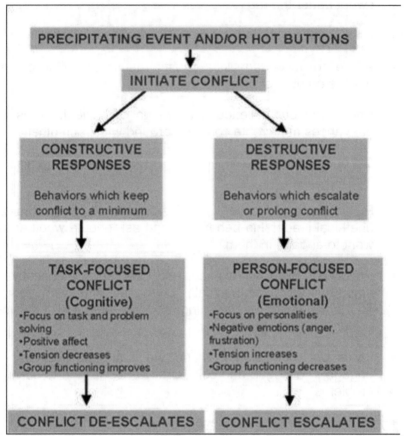

Figure 4.2 – Choosing constructive versus destructive paths to conflict resolution

Chapter 5
The Role of Perceptions and the Six Stages of Conflict Resolution

There is only one truth, steadfast, healing, salutary, and that is the absurd.[1]

Overview

A conflict has characteristics of its own, and it is possible to analyze its structure and behavior. When conflict is understood, it's easier to find ways to predict it, prevent it, transform it, and resolve it.

The way professional organizations are organized can influence both the root causes of conflict and the conditions in which these conflicts are likely to occur. Any professional organization which is organized so that some people are treated unequally and unjustly (i.e., by professional ranking, different fringe benefits and working schedules, cultural factors, and so on) is likely to erupt into conflict, especially if its leaders do not represent all the members of that organization. If an unequal and unjust society is reformed, then conflicts will be less frequent. In such situations, professional conflict mediation, and even arbitration, might be required.

As discussed thus far, any human being has basic needs, and each of us would like to be recognized as an individual and a professional with a personal identity. We all want to feel safe also. When these basic needs are not met, we protest, and protesting can create conflicts and lead to rebellion and violence. Many of us find our identity and security in our cultural groups and the particular points of view of such groups – for example, Brazilian groups are a

---

[1] Andrew Salmon (2005) *Marswalk One: First Steps on a New Planet,* *Springer.*

lot different than American and German groups! So, clashes between professionals of different cultural background are quite common and can lead to conflicts that can easily turn violent. If people learn to understand that differing cultures are not inevitably a threat to each other, they will also learn how to manage their differences co-operatively and peacefully.

Additionally, there are three dynamics that the wheel of conflict model does not include, because they cut across all the sources and are often best analyzed in terms of those sources. They are culture, power, and data. Culture affects conflict because it is embedded in individuals' communication styles, history, and way of dealing with emotions, values, and structures. Power is a very elusive concept, one that can confuse our thinking or help us understand an interaction. Some sources of power are structural, but other elements are involved as well. At MGCG, I deal with power and culture very often, especially when consulting overseas, such as in South America, the Middle East and the Pacific Rim. In my experience, data themselves are never a source of conflict, but how data are handled and communicated can lead to conflict. Therefore, data can be viewed as an issue within both communication and structure.

The Scale of Human Needs

At the core of any conflict model are the human needs that drive people's actions, including engagement in conflict. Many theorists, from Freud to Maslow, have characterized fundamental human needs. Several of them describe the different levels of needs that people experience. In the literature on conflict, a distinction is often made between interests and needs. Interests are viewed as more transitory and superficial, needs as more basic and enduring. Sometimes it is argued that resolutions that address interests but not needs are less meaningful; they are more like Band-Aids than real solutions.

Rather than conceiving of interests and needs as fundamentally different, which could be misleading and polarizing, I find it more useful to think of a continuum of human needs, roughly paralleling Maslow's hierarchy. Interests then become a category of human needs that exists between the basic concern for survival at one end of the continuum and the striving for identity at the other. Survival needs seem self-evident, so I focus here on interests and identity needs.

The statistics of war, as depicted in Figure 5.1, are so appalling that they raise a question everyone must contemplate: are such levels of suffering, imposed by conflicts amongst people, really necessary? Aren't there better ways of managing and resolving the conflicts people, and groups of people, have with each other?

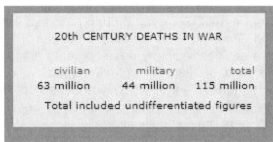

20th CENTURY DEATHS IN WAR

civilian   military   total
63 million   44 million   115 million

Total included undifferentiated figures

Figure 5.1 – The ultimate result of conflicts: 20Th Century deaths in war

By now we all should agree that conflict is a characteristic of human existence and ever present in any professional organization. It is part of the dynamic of professional endeavors that drives us into innovation and change. But it needs to be managed constructively. Hopefully, in Chapter 4 we realized that each one of us tends to have a conflict resolution style, and that at times, it may be appropriate to change our style, so that goals can be achieved. But a person with a tendency to avoid conflicts (avoidance style) will not likely be able to shift onto a competing style and become more assertive. By the same token, a person with a compromising style may not be willing to avoid a conflict, in the hopes there might be a solution for the issue,.This person might feel this way even in cases involving aggressive and violent interactions, when it is very likely no compromise can be reached. In such situation, mediation may be necessary, beginning by self-mediation.

Consider this scenario: Two coworkers are working together on a project and soon find themselves in a conflict over whether they are each pulling their weight and passing along important information to each other. In the heat of the moment they engage in a public shouting match, and each start complaining to their manager. The manager meets with them both, and they agree on a work breakdown structure and certain behavioral rules (dos and don'ts), to which they seem willing to adhere. Do you think the conflict has been resolved?

The conflict may have been alleviated along with their behavior, but each goes away from this meeting feeling victimized by the other and unappreciated by the manager. One of the coworkers decides that these feelings just result from the nature of the job and believes that the conflict has been resolved, but the other continues to see the conflict being very much alive every time the other coworker fails in any way, such as coming late for a meeting or sending an abrupt e-mail. So, even though progress has been made in the behavioral dimension, the emotional dimension is, if anything, worse, and there are contradictory developments along the cognitive dimension. This kind of result is actually typical in conflict, and it drives people to behave in apparently inconsistent ways. These coworkers may cease their overtly conflictive behavior, but the tension between them may actually increase.

But before we can discuss what mediation really is and how we can go about mediating conflicts, we must first understand the life cycle of a conflict, and what to expect, regardless of the conflict style of the parties involved, when a conflict arises.

The Role of Perceptions

Conflicts have many roots, and there are many theories that try to explain these origins. Conflict is seen as arising from basic human instincts, from the competition for resources and power, from the structure of the societies and institutions people create, and from the inevitable struggle between classes. Even though there is something to be said for most of these theories, they are not always helpful to us as we contend with conflict.

Some conflicts cannot be resolved without addressing identity-based needs. In these cases, conflicts are often not acquiescent to a negotiation process and usually require an incremental process of change in which people, teams, or organizations gradually achieve a different level of understanding and improved communication. They also often require a social change effort or a personal growth experience of some kind. Conciliation efforts in which the focus is more on the relationship among disputants and less on achieving a specific agreement may succeed in addressing these deeper needs.

It is not useful to argue whether it is less valuable or meaningful to work on interests than to address identity-based needs. Our work should focus on conflict in a sequenced and compromising way because only through progress at more accessible level can agreements be made at a deeper level. Sometimes, deeper levels of needs are simply not involved in significant ways. If a resolution process genuinely addresses needs people have in a way that is meaningful to them, then important progress has been made.

The role of perception in conflicts is very strong and must be considered before any attempt of mediation is in place. Actually, such perception will impact the conflict itself, as most conflicts, in their first stages, are "perceived" conflicts in our own minds, based on our own cultural, educational and social filters and idiosyncrasies. Figure 5.2 illustrates how perceptual filters can immensely define and affect the object of conflict between two parties.

Figure 5.2 – The role of perceptions in conflicts

Our responses to conflicts can be emotional, cognitive, or physical:

- **Emotional**: The feelings we experience in conflict, such as anger, fear, despair, and confusion. Often misunderstood;

people tend to think others feel the same as they do. Emotional responses can also be threatening.

- **Cognitive**: Our ideas and thoughts about a conflict. Often present as inner voices (self-talk) in the midst of a situation, we may come to understand these cognitive responses.

- **Physical**: Include heightened stress, bodily tension, increased perspiration, tunnel vision, shallow or accelerated breathing, nausea, and rapid heartbeat.

There many cognitive and emotional factors outlined in Figure 5.2 conspire to form the perceptual filters through which we experience conflicts. More specifically here it is how these factors impact our perception of a conflict:

- **Previous experiences**, as illustrated in Figure 5.3, taps onto out profound and significant life experiences, and continues to influence our perceptions of current situations. Past experiences may have left us fearful, lacking trust, and reluctant to take risks, or the opposite!!

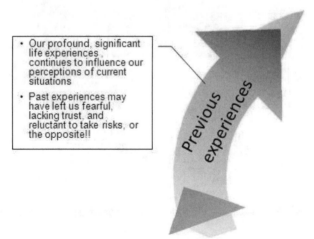

Figure 5.3 – How previous experiences affect how we experience a conflict.

- **The messenger**, as illustrated in Figure 5.4, can be perceived as a powerful, scary, or unknown, as a threat. The way you perceive your boss delivering a bad news, or some information that causes you fear or threats you can influence your responses to the overall situation being experienced.

It is very typical for employees who had abusive or authoritative parents, for example, to overreact to a directive given by a supervisor, if that supervisor resembles the parent. The messenger, more than the message, is the cause of conflict here.

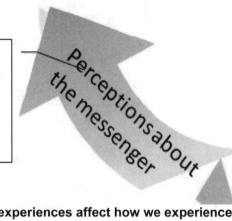

- Do you perceive the messenger as a threat (powerful, scary, unknown, etc.)?
- Perceptions can influence our responses to the overall situation being experienced.

Figure 5.4 – How previous experiences affect how we experience a conflict.

- **Knowledge**, as illustrated in Figure 5.5, both general and situational, tends to drive our responses to conflicts. Statements such as "Do I understand what is going on here?" points to a situation-specific knowledge, while "Have I experienced this type of situation before?" points to a general knowledge about the issue.

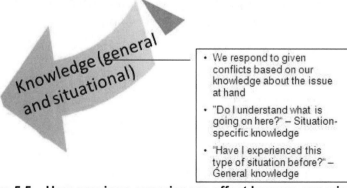

- We respond to given conflicts based on our knowledge about the issue at hand
- "Do I understand what is going on here?" – Situation-specific knowledge
- "Have I experienced this type of situation before?" – General knowledge

Figure 5.5 – How previous experiences affect how we experience a conflict.

63

- **Gender and sexuality**, as illustrated in Figure 5.6, is also significant in the way we perceive conflicts, as men and women often perceive situations differently (such as power and privilege, as do different races and ethnicities). In addition, socialization patterns, such as relationships versus task, substance versus process, and immediacy versus long-term outcomes will also affect how we perceive conflicts.

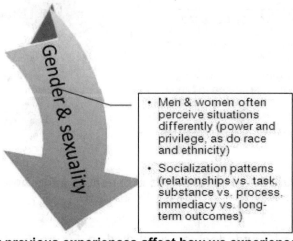

Figure 5.6 – How previous experiences affect how we experience a conflict.

- **Culture, race, and ethnicity**, as illustrated in Figure 5.7, is of great impact on perceptions as varying cultural backgrounds influence our beliefs, our social structures and the role of conflict in it. We may have different views on substantive, procedural, and psychological values and needs, which may affect negotiation and conflict management

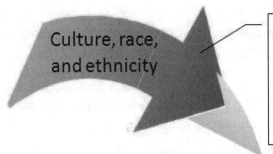

Culture, race, and ethnicity

- Varying cultural background influence our believes, of social structures at work and the role of conflict in it.
- We may have different views on substantive, procedural, and psychological values and needs, which may affect negotiation and conflict management

Figure 5.7 – How previous experiences affect how we experience a conflict.

The Life-cycle of a Conflict

Regardless of the emotional and physical aspects of a conflict, any and every conflict is a process, a cluster of events taking time to evolve and reshape. Of course, conflicts are constantly complicated. But there are, nonetheless, distinct stages that every conflict goes through, which are very important for you to understand and be able to identify, so you can recognize them and react accordingly, especially if you are a part of the conflict.

These stages are common to all conflicts, and they all pass through it, sometimes over and over again. Understanding each stage of a conflict is, therefore, paramount in enabling you to identify the conflict and attempt to resolve it.

How Does Conflict Resolution Work?

Most conflict resolution strategies follow a series of steps that typically include:

1. **Establishment of ground rules** – An agreement to work together and set rules of engagement (i.e. no swearing, blaming, yelling, hitting, or interrupting).

2. **Active listening** – Each party on the conflict has the chance to describe their point of view, without interruption, or interpretations. The point is to understand what a person wants (the needs) and why they want it, as well as any perceived fear or threats.

3. **Identifying common interests** - Establish facts and issues that everyone can agree on and determine what is important to each person, their interests, values, and needs.

4. **Brainstorming** - List all potential solutions without judging them or feeling that they must be carried out. Try to think of solutions where everyone gains something.

5. **Negotiation** - Negotiate and try to reach a compromise that is acceptable to everyone involved.

6. **Reaching agreement**. Each person should state his or her interpretation of the agreement. You should then try to write up a draft of the agreement, get the parties to review it, and then, sometime later, check back with them to see how it is working.

The Beginning: Stage One

Every conflict is born out of the differences between the conflicting parties, especially when people start taking sides. In this stage you can quickly detect language embedded with "you and I," instead of "us," or "us and them" instead of "we." Also, the idea of a "cause" to support begins to emerge on both sides. It is important to note that there is no violence (i.e., harsh words, aggressive tones, or even physical aggression) at this point.

If a team is strong and its leaders enlightened, a conflict can be dealt with in a constructive and positive way at this early stage, and violence and a worsening situation can be avoided.

Early Escalation: Stage Two

If there are no existing ways of dealing with conflicts at an organization, such as policies and procedures, training, or the availability of mediation or arbitration, the conflict will grow worse. At this stage it is common to see the two sides of the conflict expressing open hostility. The language may change from "us and them," to some variation of "the adversary," or "the enemy."

From this point on, each side increases its demands, and its sense of grievance swells. Each side looks for allies from outside the conflict area, for moral and physical support. It is here, at this stage, that acts of violence begin, which can vary from a slight increase of voice, to verbal abuse, from confrontational demeanor to actual physical violence. If violence is not repressed, the opposing sides will hit back at one another and a destructive and deadly spiral may begin.

If one of the sides has greater forces (as one of the parties being backed by a manager, or a department head) it may at this stage suppress its opponents, but the underlying causes of conflict will remain to break out another day.

Reaching a Deadlock: Stage Three

At this stage, both sides are at war, very likely a "loud" war! Each counterpart of the conflict perceives the other as the aggressor to whom blame for the conflict should be attributed.   Each counterpart of the conflict believes he or she is right, that his or her cause is correct. The lawlessness of open conflict, or "civilized war" if you may, takes over, as inhibitions and restraints on violence are abandoned. At this point, there are three possible situations that might be reached:

- A stalemate with each side matching the other in violence

- A surge of violence on one side, or

- Exhaustion of strength and resources on both sides, in which case three possible scenarios arise:

  a) The interactions between the parties involved continues to spiral into violence, or may even halt at some particular level where both sides retain their opinions and position;

  b) There may be an opportunity for change, where, for instance, one of the counterparts increased power may cause the other side to change its tactics. This by no means indicates the resolution of the conflict, which may subside back to its early stages and will be prone to repeat itself. It will be just a matter of time (and opportunity) for the conflict to begin again later.

c) This is the position from which the conflict can most readily move to its next stage: stage four.

Looking for a Way out: Stage Four

There will be a point in a conflict where both sides will just no longer be able to tolerate all the side effects brought by the conflict. Examples of such effects may include unhappiness about things being lost (such as time, joy, opportunities, respect, friendships, etc.), decreasing resources, and lack of attainable results.

At this point, there is a very likely possibility that the parties in conflict may enter into a sort of truce agreement. Such strategy provides a pause, which is often used for resting and regrouping before going back and embarking on the earlier stages of the conflict again. It is just a matter of time, and sooner or later, both sides will decide that the best alternative is to end the conflict. At this stage, the concern now is to do it in such a way without losing face. Possible alternatives may include the introduction of a mediator, or arbitrator, to attempt to negotiate the issue.

There will be times when you will not be able to negotiate any type of compromise, as the other party may not be open for any deal. While the best situation is when both parties are interested in negotiating a solution to the conflict, sometimes it won't be possible. In this case, if you can transform the situation into one where the person not willing to negotiate recognizes the potential benefits of a negotiated agreement, and compromise at least, it may be helpful. This is how these conflict resolution stages can help: By focusing first on listening to the other person, and seeking to understand the sources of their resistance, you can then set the stage for clarifying the conditions he or she requires in order to talk things out, to come up to some sort of agreement. This isn't about being "right" or "'wrong" in the situation, but a practical strategy for getting the other person engaged as a partner in the negotiation process.

However, the other person may still resist the idea of negotiating a solution! In such situations, shift away from substantive needs and focus first on procedural needs to be negotiated. Remember that procedural needs are those that relate to the process we are using to negotiate. Another alternative is to focus on things we can do to influence conflicts in the future, rather than putting initial energy into understanding (or solving) problems we have had in the past. By remaining relatively flexible about the agenda - taking on topics you care about, but not necessarily the most pressing issues - you create an opportunity to reduce the fears associated with resistance. While you may not be able to truly resolve the conflicts, you will still be able to manage some of the key issues that exist and prevent those issues from getting worse.

Resolving the Conflict: Stage Five

Settling a conflict and resolving it is not the same thing. Settling a conflict will require you to compromise to one extent or another. The compromising process in itself is often sprinkled with bitter arguments over what the compromises will be, seldom leading to a solution in which the two sides can collaborate to establish a firm peace and resolution. In addition, settlements should also establish ways in which the contenders are prepared to end the conflict at least for the time being.

Conflict resolution, on the other hand, takes into consideration the underlying causes that started the conflict and deals with them. This is important, so the risks of future conflicts occurring again are removed, or at least reduced. Both sides join together to achieve this outcome. Unfortunately, after much hostility and hurts that typically result from conflicts, complete resolutions are difficult to attain, but quite possible after a time of reconnection, healing, and trust building, if everyone has the same goal in mind.

Types of conflict resolution programs

- Conflict-resolution training programs are often taught as separate courses in schools and communities.

- Peer-mediation programs teach teens to serve as mediators and resolve conflicts among their peers.

- Peaceable classrooms and schools incorporate conflict resolution into classroom teaching and throughout the school environment.

- Community mediation centers train community volunteers to provide mediation services to youth and adults. Some centers may also train youth to become mediators.

Working Together: Stage Six

At this stage, the agreement has to be put into effect, and each side needs to create a new set of goals together. Even more important, each side needs to look into the past, own their actions and the results of such actions, share their grief, and reconcile their differences. This is a very important stage, and the most difficult one, as it requires sensitivity, courage, and, above all, immense patience.

Heuristic Approach to Conflict Resolution

No matter how you approach and deploy the six stages of conflict resolution, if you are a party to the conflict or a mediator, make sure to keep in mind these heuristic (rule of thumb!) approaches to resolving a conflict:

- **Be calm and do not speak in anger** – If necessary, take some time off to cool off before expressing your point of view, but don't express it in anger. The last thing you want is for people to react to your emotions and anger, and not listen to your message.

- **Be careful when choosing the location and the time for mediation sessions** – Make sure to select a place and time carefully. You should avoid confrontations in public, or around people that are not part of the conflict. Try to select a good time to meet with the other party, or parties, in the conflict to discuss the issue. Keep in mind that some of us function better early in the day, which others do well in the evening. I tend to be a night owl, and therefore, am very foggy early on the day. Avoid emotional or difficult times, such as when the other person is dealing with a loss or mistake, at the end of a hard day, or when in a hurry or working under a deadline.

- **Calmly present your concerns** – If necessary, you might want to take notes of what you want to say, or must say, so you can stay on course and not take "side trips" during your communication with the opposing party.

- **Compromise, even if for a time** – Finally, when a conflict remains unresolved, you may decide to let it go or to continue to pursue an acceptable resolution. If you choose the latter, communicate with the person at the next level and ask for advice and assistance.

- **Give the other party a chance to express him or herself** - Some people are very open and extroverted, quick to say what they think. Others are not, being introverted and requiring a bit more of time to process their comments and concerns, and to formulate a response.

- **It is not what you say but how you say it** – Avoid by all means finger-pointing, blame-shift, or accusations. A very important strategy in conflict resolution is the depersonalization of your comments. Focus on the issue, not on you or them. Be aware of your (and their!) body language, eye contact, gestures, facial expression, tone inflection and volume when discussing issues with him/her. Conflict resolution becomes more difficult when the involved parties are responding defensively.

- **Keep on trying** - If the response to your concerns is unacceptable or if there is no response at all, try again.

- **Listen carefully** - Give the other person your complete attention. It is not enough to hear, you must listen!

- **Put yourself in their shoes** - Try to understand the other person's behavior from her/his viewpoint, by expressing your understanding of the other position. This will demonstrate that you are not only concerned with your own point of view, but also the other side, which may help open up communication.

Chapter 6
Conflict Mediation

If people around you are spiteful, callous, and will not hear you, fall down before them and beg for their forgiveness; for in truth you are to blame for their not wanting to hear you.[1]

Overview

According to Carol Watson and Richard Hoffman[2] more than 42% of managers' time is spent on reaching an agreement when conflict occurs. As discussed earlier, we manage people, and people are motivated. As motivated people our nature compels us into conflict. So, it will not be unusual if you have not been in a position where you had to manage a conflict between one or more people in your group, department, or in the company.

Most importantly, according to Daniel Dana, in his book Conflict Resolution,[3] it has been estimated that over 60% of performance deficiencies result from problems in employee's relationships, not from problems with individuals. The question is: What would you do, if two members of your team were in a conflict and you could not afford to lose either of them? Typically most organizations would try to transfer one of the employees to another department, but such a strategy typically means the loss of technical skills, since replacements would probably mean new hires, which would require extensive one-on-one training; or hiring someone that would not be abreast of the issues at hand.

So what are your options? Well, any MBA textbook would give you some suggestions, such as:

- Breakup - As mentioned earlier, you could send one of the professionals in the conflict to another department, reducing the amount of time they interact and preventing, therefore,

---

[1] Dostoevsky, *The Brothers Karamazov*
[2] "Managers as Negotiators," *The Leadership Quarterly* 7 (1), 1996
[3] 2001, McGraw-Hill

further conflicts. But we know that such an approach inevitably will produce inefficiencies and lack of performance, especially if they were all part of the same team

- Counseling and coaching a team can go a long way, and so does training them proactively in conflict resolution, teambuilding, and decision-making processes. A good portion of my consulting practice at MGCG is precisely on training and coaching in these areas. But counseling is not always directed at the source of the conflict. A well-meaning coaching session can get out of hand as it delves into the problem, and the counselor may appear to be taking sides, even if he or she intends to stay neutral, and may become someone's opponent.

- Ignore - I would not count on this but sometimes conflicts can go away all by themselves

- Termination of employment is the most drastic approach one can take to resolve a conflict. You can get rid of feuding employees completely, but it will be very likely one of the most costly and strategies you may choose, as you will have to hire a new professional, train him or her, and bring she or he up to speed

- Use of coercion - People tend to respond to coercion if their basic needs depend on it (i.e., need for a paycheck, need to belong in the group or organization, desire to learn, etc.), but many will become even less cooperative.

Therefore, it is usually a good idea for you to discuss the pros and cons of the options with a human resource professional at your organization or with an expert, a consultant, or a professional outsider not from your department or group, who would likely give you an unbiased advice into the issue. But, again, do not assume that they know about all the options or that they have the solution for your problem. Your best approach would be mediation. Management mediation is still new to many human resource professionals. This is the topic of this chapter.

There are over 200 conflict mediation programs across the United States and around the world. About 80 to 85 percent of cases that go to mediation result in a mutually agreeable resolution. There are more conflict mediation definitions and approaches than are suitable to this book, but in general, you should view conflict mediation as an excellent alternative for a confidential and voluntary process that aims to reach win/win solutions for people and teams who are in conflict with each other. Trained mediators facilitate a transformative mediation process to:

- Encourage face to face dialogue

- Discuss concerns and issues

- Build understanding

- Search for win/win solutions

Mediation at Work

Mastering basic mediation skills can take your professional life (and career) to the next level. Philosophically, litigation and mediation seem worlds apart. While both are forms of conflict resolution that involve an outside party, the outcomes differ wildly. The results of litigation rarely satisfy both parties. The results of mediation are far more satisfying, since mediators use negotiation skills (more on this in Chapter 7) to reach a common ground on which all parties can agree.

In a nutshell, mediation is a way of reframing a situation, or conflict, in order to persuade the people in conflict to shift their positions so as to make a resolution possible. To be a successful mediator you need to understand some basics about human behavior and practice the fine art of paying attention.

There are three levels, or phases, in the mediation process, namely a pre-mediation, mediation, and follow up.

Pre-Mediation Phase

In pre-mediation, once the parties involved in the conflict agree to participate in the mediation process, one or two mediators are engaged in the process. It is always good to have two mediators involved in the process as a fall back, in case of conflict, and so that they can operate in tandem, as a sounding board, but there is no absolute need to have two mediators. But if you work with two mediators, these co-mediators should schedule a separate pre-mediation meeting with each party involved in the conflict. The purpose of this meeting is to find out more about the conflict at hand and that party's perspective. This is also a good time to address any questions or issues about the process.

Mediation Phase

In the mediation stage, the parties in conflict would meet for the mediation session. The location should be outside their organization, a public but quiet place, or the mediator's office. This is, if you recall from earlier discussion, to promote a safe and conducive environment to discuss the conflict and its issues. Each party should have an opportunity to tell his/her perspective. The mediators should listen and guide the process to facilitate increased understanding between the parties. The mediators should then use problem-solving techniques, some already discussed here, aimed to assist participants reach win/win solutions, or at minimum a compromise. The mediation session usually tends to last a few hours (2-3 hours). Most conflicts tend to be resolved within one or two mediation sessions.

Follow-up Phase

The mediator should then follow up with all parties approximately three months after mediation to make sure agreements reached are being followed. This follow up may consist of calling the parties to see how things are going since the conclusion of the mediation.

Conflict Resolution Process through Self-Mediation

To summarize what we have discussed thus far, and before we get into conflict mediation, there are eight useful steps that can aid you in effectively managing conflicts. These steps cannot guarantee that you will arrive at an agreement, but it can greatly improve the likelihood of problems being understood and solutions being explored, and consideration of the advantages of a negotiated agreement can occur within a relatively constructive environment.

The first four steps, as depicted in Figure 6.1, can greatly assist you resolving conflicts, beginning by:

1. **Knowing yourself**, knowing your strengths as a professional, but also what you bring to the table in dealing with this conflict. Typical attributes may include patience, consideration for your fellow co-worker, training in conflict resolution, etc. You also need to know your weaknesses, or if you prefer, what are your "hot buttons"? Typical attributes here may be lack of patience, guilt or knowing you are at fault, lack of communication skills, being emotional, etc.

   It might be worthwhile for you to know what opportunities you see in attempting to resolve the conflict. From negotiation one-on-one we learn about knowing your BATNA, or your "best alternative to negotiating agreements."

   If you know what your "bottom-line" is, you will be better prepared to enter an agreement, or not. Lastly, know what threatens you. What are your fears based on? Do you fear termination of employment/contract? Maybe you fear losing your reputation, your respect, or learning that you are wrong (or even that you are right!). Without being cognitive of your fears you will not be able to proactively engage in a conflict resolution exercise.

   After all, you must take care of yourself and make sure not to hurt yourself with dynamics that are destructive.

2. **Clarify needs**, by conveying to your opponent what the needs (or fears) you feel are being threatened by the conflict. It is very important that the person(s) you are having a conflict with are very clear about what the issues are. But it is also very important that you certify that your issues both perceived ones as your own, are not only a perception, but that they are real.

3. **Identify a safe place** to discuss your issues, to work out the conflict. It will be prudent to move the discussion outside of the working premises. Not only it will be a safer environment where the two of you, or the group can freely talk about the issues, but if the conflict escalates, at least you have protected the interests of those in conflict, as well as the organization.

Also, it should be a place where you know you will not be interrupted, a place that is not threatening in any way to any of the parties in the conflict. It should be a neutral place.

4. **Listen well** - Really make sure to invest time in listening, and listen well. One of the most difficult tasks in conflict resolution is to listen to someone who is going against you, does not agree with you, threatens you, and is not meeting your needs. But if you listen well, chances are your perceptions of the conflict will be more realistic, less emotionally based.

If you listen, you will be cognitive of what you don't understand (take mental notes, or write it down, don't interject, don't interrupt when someone is speaking), and will have a chance to clarify the issue before you have a chance to address your issues. Your goal in listening is to understand, not to retaliate. Your goal in listening is to try to collaborate, to compromise, if necessary. Your goal is not to generate rapid-fire responses to what is being said.

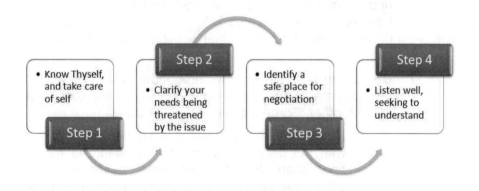

Figure 6.1 – First four basic steps in resolving conflicts

The four steps above comprise the first stage where the issues are placed on the table, where both contenders in the conflict have a chance to portray what the issue is, how they feel about the issue(s) and have also a chance to hear the other party on those very same issues, from the other point of view. If done well, you now can move onto the second half of the conflict resolution process, as depicted in Figure 6.2. The next four steps in this process entail:

5. **Clarify your needs**, by asserting them clearly and concisely. In light of your threatened needs and fears, and after listening to your opponents' point of view on the issue, what are your real needs? Are they the same as you started with, or did they change?

   Clearly and briefly express your needs, your bottom-line. Again, be all ears when it is your opponent's turn.

6. **Be flexible!** Very unlikely, unless there was a misperception or misconception with regards to the conflict, your way or your opponent's way will not be so attractive to each other.

   Try not to focus on who is right, or who is entitled to their needs. Instead, try to view the issue from the perspective of *what* is right, *what* is fair. In this process, you might want to ask yourself and your opponent what is the last point of agreement between the two of you. Try to work from that point on.
   Keep your negotiation efforts focused on reconciliation, and not on winning or saving face. It will take humility from here on; it will take also a lot of courage to give in, to concede, without feeling that you are weak, or that you lost.

7. **Be patient**. Especially throughout the negotiation process, make sure to remain calm, patient and respectful to each other. Some techniques may include:

   a. Make sure to establish a good personal rapport with the person you are dealing with. No matter how sharp the disagreements, never let them affect the personal relationship. Because in the final analysis, you need good will in order to clinch a deal.

   b. Learn to "read" people. In order to do that you must become a good listener, so you can pick up the nuances, body language and clues to help you find a way forward.

c. A sense of humor goes a long way. Conflicts can be extremely tense. When people are tense, they clam up. But they also laugh easily. Laughter relieves the tension and can get the discussion moving again.

d. It is never what you say, but how you say it. Present your case in terms that are palatable to the other side. Avoid the temptation to score too many debating points. The negotiator's tools are the stiletto, not the hammer; they are the shoe horn, not the chain saw.

8. **Build an agreement**, one that works! Whatever agreement you develop, make sure to build an agreement that is reasonable, realistic, that works!

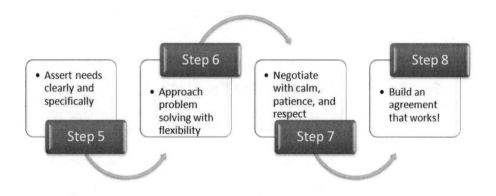

Figure 6.2 – Second half of the conflict resolution process

Mediating Conflicts

In the role of manager as mediator, the main strategies for success include:

- Make sure to keep the team, or group, involved in the conflict and engaged in this initial process

- Support conciliatory gestures, such as verbal statements that expose your vulnerability and willingness to have the situation resolved. Here is a short list of kinds of conciliatory gesture that you may use:

- Apologizing
- Conceding
- Expressing positive feelings for the other
- Initiating a win-win approach to the problem.
- Owning responsibility
- Self-disclosing

This short self-assessment can help you in identifying reconciliatory attitudes for resolving conflicts and helping others in conflicts through mediation:

1. What actions can you take to avoid blaming and punishing?

   _____
   _____
   _____
   _____

2. How can you improve the conflict situation?

   _____
   _____
   _____
   _____

3. How can you improve the communication of your feelings appropriately?

   _____
   _____
   _____
   _____

4. How can you improve the relationship with the opponents and increase your level of communication?

   _____
   _____
   _____
   _____

5. How can you avoid repeating the same situation and entering into the same conflict in the future?

_____

_____

_____

_____

6. If communication is not appropriate, what other action(s) can I take?

_____

_____

_____

_____

Mediating Emotions

People behave and enter into conflict for a purpose. They are looking for ways to belong, feel significant, and self-protect. As discussed earlier, when people perceive a threat to their self-esteem, a downhill spiral can begin. People can be led into obstructive behaviors in the faulty belief that this will gain them a place of belonging and significance. How we respond to their difficult behaviors can determine how entrenched these become.

People in a conflict should have opportunities to develop knowledge and understanding of themselves, and how to handle and react appropriately to the range of conflicts they are facing. They should have opportunities to develop knowledge and understanding of conflict in a variety of contexts and how to respond to it positively and creatively. In addition, they should have opportunities to develop an informed awareness of the similarities and differences between the cultural traditions which can influence contenders in a conflict, and of international and transnational influences on contemporary culture.

When mediating such people, your goal should be to break out of the spiral by supporting their real needs without supporting their destructive faulty beliefs, and alienating patterns of reaction. Table 6.1 summarizes the issues.

Table 6.1 – Mediating Emotions

Mediating Emotions		
Difficult Behavior (and the Faulty Belief Behind It)	**The downhill Spiral**	**Better Alternatives**
Seeking Attention: "I only belong when I am being noticed."	The person feels annoyed and reacts by coaxing. They stop briefly, and then resume behavior and demands,, perhaps in a new way.	Avoid undue attention. Give attention for positive behavior especially when they are not making a bid for it. Support their real contribution and involvement.
Power Plays: "I only belong when I am in control, when no-one can boss me!"	You feel provoked or threatened and react by fighting or giving in. Their aggression is intensified or they comply defiantly.	Disengage from the struggle. Help them to use power constructively by enlisting co-operation. Support their self-worth and autonomy.
Seeking Revenge: "I am significant only if I make others feel hurt like I do."	You feel hurt by them, and retaliate. They seek further revenge more strongly or with another weapon	Convince them that you respect their needs. Build trusting relationships. Support their need for justice and fairness.
Appear Inadequate: "I won't be hurt any more, only if I can convince others not to expect much from me."	You give up, overwhelmed. They respond passively, show no improvement, and stay the "victim".	Encourage any positive effort, no matter how small. Focus on assets. Provide modest opportunities for success. Support feelings as a starting place for self-improvement.

Chapter 7
Negotiating Conflicts

Conflict is inevitable, but combat is optional.[1]

Overview

Many professionals could dramatically improve their work environment and team work by learning to negotiate conflicts effectively, without bumping into conflict of interests, as illustrated in Figure 7.1. For instance, learning to negotiate a conflict would help them deal with demanding, disgruntled coworkers and go back to work on more productive tasks and projects. It would also help them negotiate with opposing team workers to reach concessions and agreements that can save time and money by reducing the issues in dispute or even settling the case. In addition, they could be better able to help their peers become more willing to negotiate their conflicts.

> **❝ It's almost impossible to give the seller the highest and best price for a home and help the buyer purchase that same home for the lowest amount.
> It's a conflict. ❞**

Figure 7.1 – Watch out for conflicts of interests!

Coworkers or clients who are angry or feel hurt in some way may not always be willing to accept an agreement that is not in line

---

[1] *Max Lucado (2007) Dealing with difficult people, Thomas Nelson*

with their interests or needs. There comes a point, often after a stalemate is reached, as depicted in Figure 7.2, where the parties decide to try negotiation to resolve the conflict. The process of initiating negotiation can be difficult as it may be interpreted as a sign of weakness. This is one reason why it is often useful for mediators to become involved in the negotiation process.

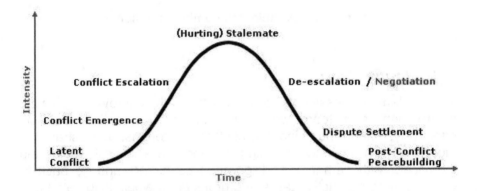

Figure 7.2 – Watch out for conflicts of interests!

The timing of such a step is very important. Conflict resolution can only be achieved if the parties are willing to negotiate. In order for the conditions to be favorable, there must be both a perception on all sides that the present course is unsustainable, and a perception that there is a suitable "way out" of the conflict. In some ways, the parties in conflict realize their course of action cannot succeed, and they become more willing to negotiate. But there are times that mediation becomes necessary.

The timing is critical, however, because if conflict negotiation begins too early, before both parties are ready, it is likely to fail. And repeated failed negotiation efforts reinforce the notion that the conflict is intractable and can make resolution more difficult by discouraging further efforts. Conflict negotiation may lead to a settlement, but may also simply lead to a compromise, or even a truce in the conflict. If the latter, there is a relatively good chance the conflict will cycle back to escalation at a later time.

Conflict negotiations typically go through a series of stages: first, each group decides on its position; then each determines its best alternative to negotiating an agreement (BATNA); its mediator(s); and its agenda. Once together with the other party, they share their positions, consider options, exchange concessions, perhaps reach an accord, and implement it.

A number of theories have emerged to understand negotiating tactics, their strengths and weaknesses, as well as how to respond to them. Typically though, negotiations are complex, drawn-out processes and a broad range of factors make each one somewhat unique. Their shape depends upon the procedures that have become institutionalized, the number of parties and number of representatives present, the scope of issues under discussion, the degree to which it is part of a broader framework of negotiations, and the extent to which they are taking place in the public eye.

The following is a list of strategies, similar to conflict mediation strategies, but with the focus of negotiating an agreement (one of the last stages in conflict mediation):

- **Behind a wall of silence there is always a strong emotion** - I had an experience once at a power generation company where one of the workers was not willing to accept the recommendations we were about to provide to their project management group, so that their projects could be more successfully executed. As a powerful stakeholder, he was about to walk into the senior management office and let them know he was not going to endorse such intervention and not allow any budget allocation for such a task. When anyone, including some of my associates tried to talk to him about his issues, he gave terse emotionless answers. So during a private meeting I asked him what he wanted to achieve. He almost broke down, saying, "I never wanted to bring this case in the first place. I just want to be heard by upper management, I want my opinion to matter."

  So I went back to upper management and asked if this manager's opinions were ever asked about the project management issues and mentioned the fact he was also contributing to fund this intervention. Upper management had proposed the solution at a big staff meeting, with not much time for all parties to be heard before a vote, where most of the managers present agreed to hire a consultant to look into the lack of project management best practices. They called him out for a lunch, I joined them, he expressed his concerns, they listened attentively, and by the time dessert was served his support was granted, unconditionally! This illustrates how tapping into repressed emotions can lead to a solution that makes everyone happy.

- **Identify the real impediment in every conflict** – When negotiating conflicts, ask yourself "What is the real motivation behind this issue?" Once you identify the real impediment, you should be able to predict how your client will respond and then shape the negotiations accordingly. I once worked on a wrongful termination case where the plaintiff employee refused to settle. One day I happened to ask about his family. He told me one of his kids had cerebral palsy. Suddenly, I understood why he felt it necessary to win the case: he didn't have medical insurance to cover his child's medical treatments. Armed with knowledge of what was driving the lawsuit, I spoke to an officer of the company, who agreed to have the company pay the plaintiff's health insurance for five years.

- **Become a mind reader** - Mind reading is not magic. It's a combination of observation, listening, intuition and experience. Observing body language and listening closely, not only to what clients say but also to the emotional tone of their words, can reveal a lot about what your clients think. Ask your clients to talk about themselves (most will gladly do so). This will provide information about their perspectives and create openings for questions. Once you have the information you need, you should be able to anticipate how your clients might react to certain developments in the case.

Here it is a little exercise to make my point on mind reading:

1. Think of a number between 1 and 10

2. Multiple that number by 9

3. Add the two digits together

4. Take away 5

5. Translate that into a letter of the alphabet – A for 1, B for 2, C for 3, D for 4, E for 5, F for 6, etc.

6. Now think of a country that starts with that letter

7. Take the second letter of that country and think of a big animal that starts with that letter

Now, as illustrated in Figure 7.3, how do I know you were thinking of an *elephant in Denmark* (unless you're from the Western side of the US, in which case you probably thought about an elk)? Well if you're Latin you thought about Dominique Republic and an orangutan or ox. AND, if distracted, you probably messed up!

Figure 7.3 – The best way to predict the future is to make it!

- **Speak your opponent's, language** - Listen carefully to determine what Neuro-Linguistic Programming (NLP) "type" your client and adversary may be. According to NLP principles, there are three types of people: visual, auditory, and kinesthetic:

  o A kinesthetic person might say, "That feels right to me," or "I'm not grasping what you're telling me." A person who seems emotionally shut down is probably a kinesthetic person as well.

o   A visual person would say, "Can we look into this further?" and "I am getting a clearer picture now."

o   An auditory person might say, "I hear you loud and clear," or "Now that you've voiced your opinion, may I tell you what would resonate with me?"

This is very important because as soon as you determine what NLP category your opponent falls into, you should be able to deliberately build a rapport with him or her. Do so by using the same words and phrases that they use when you ask questions and seek out information. This will make it easier for them to respond.

- **Be creative about cooperation alternatives** - In every case, there is a tension between the desire to compete and the desire to cooperate. As a mediator, or someone trying to resolve a conflict, it is up to you to find a solution that serves you and your opponent's best interests. The goal here, as depicted in Figure 7.4, is to identify where your mutual interests lies and try to start negotiation at that point.

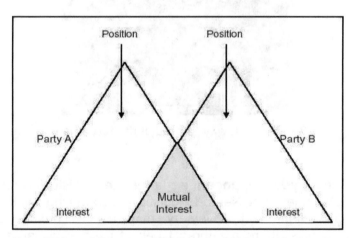

Figure 7.4 – Determining a point of mutual interest between you and your opponent

If your opponent does not know what his/her best interests are, you can use your negotiation skills to steer her in the right direction. Mediation can protect the parties in conflict from the anxiety and delays associated with litigation and save them from incurring large legal fees.

- **Retell the story if necessary** – Opponents of a conflict may tend to get stuck in their positions because they tell what happened over and over again from a narrow and negative viewpoint. They typically can't see the situation any other way without help from a mediator. When opponents are reluctant to move off of a position, preventing any forward movement, one way to motivate them, as depicted in Figure 7.5, is to retell their story in a positive, forward-looking way. This literally gives clients new words with which to see their options in a different light.

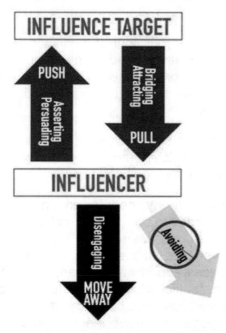

Figure 7.5 – Retelling the story of a conflict as a strategy for negotiation

As a mediator, or someone self-mediating, you are assuming a role of influencer, while the other party, or parties, of the conflict are targets of your influence. As you retell a story in a more positive tone (watch your language!), you are pushing a assertion and persuasion language onto your target, which in turn, if successful, should promote a more attracting scenario, and more bridging attitude to conflicts and negotiation. Of course, in some circumstances, you might want to move away, by disengaging.

- **Conflict negotiation is not a magic wand** – As strict organizational hierarchies become a thing of the past and organizations rely on teams to get the work done, building good relationships and cultivating influence in order to secure the results you want have become essential survival skills. Whether you're dealing with a supervisor, coworker or team member with their own managers, winning their respect and cooperation is absolutely essential for conflict mediation and resolution.

When you improve your conflict mediation skills, you will gain the ability to increase value in numerous aspects of your professional life or business simply by increasing the effectiveness of your communication skills and persuasiveness.

Conflict negotiation skills, however, will not always enable you to reach agreements. Some opponents will not budge from their opinions, no matter what you say.

- **Inspire trust** - Many people are naturally skeptical of mediators and any reconciliatory actions from the part of opponents. Everyone has heard a few good mediator jokes, and they never present mediators in a positive light. That's why it is necessary to always present yourself, mediator or a member of a conflict with reconciliatory goals in mind, in a way that communicates that they can trust you to be fair in the way you engage and treat them. Figure 7.6 provides an overview of what Robert F. Hurley[2] portrait as the ten factors for inspiring and enhancing trust.

---

[2] *Harvard Business Review* article by Robert F. Hurley, titled "The Decision to Trust," (2007).

FACTOR	TO INCREASE EMPLOYEES'...	
Risk tolerance	Faith that "things will work out"	• Spend more time explaining options during stressful times. • Offer a safety net.
Adjustment	Confidence; belief that the world is a benign place	• Recognize employee's achievements. • Correct failures through coaching, not harsh discipline.
Power	Feeling of authority	• Provide choices; avoid being coercive. • Explain how decisions serve company interests.
Security	Sense of safety	• Provide comfort during turbulent times. • Temper risks inherent in times of change.
Similarity	Sense of shared values and group identity	• Use "we" more than "I." • Emphasize what you have in common.
Interest alignment	Sense of shared interests	• Find wins for employees. • Explain how meeting company goals benefits everyone.
Benevolent concern	Belief that you will put yourself at risk for them	• Demonstrate genuine concern for employees. • Occasionally make sacrifices for employees.
Capability	Perception that you're competent	• Demonstrate your skills in relation to tasks at hand. • Delegate tasks you're not good at.
Predictability/ Integrity	Belief that you be-have consistently and fulfill promises	• Underpromise and overdeliver. • If you can't fulfill a promise, explain why.
Communication	Experience of open and honest exchanges	• Increase frequency and candor of your communications. • Cultivate bonds beyond workplace roles; e.g., by having lunch.

Figure 7.6 – Hurley's ten factors for inspiring and enhancing trust

Having Conflict Negotiation Skills

As discussed earlier, conflict negotiation is a process in which you or someone else assists in resolving a dispute between two or more parties in conflict. It is a non-adversarial approach to conflict resolution. In this role, it is very important to develop conflict negotiation skills to facilitate communication between the parties, assist them in focusing on the real issues of the dispute, and generate options that meet the interests or needs of all relevant parties in an effort to resolve the conflict.

It is very important not to confuse mediation with arbitration when attempting to negotiate a conflict. Unlike arbitration, where the intermediary listens to the arguments of both sides and makes a decision for the disputants, a mediator assists the parties to develop a solution themselves. So, in conflict negotiation via a mediator, the parties in conflict will develop their solutions and agreements, and not the mediator. Although mediators often provide ideas and suggestions, the mediator's primary role is of a process-oriented person, assisting the parties define the agenda, identify and reframe the issues, communicate more effectively and find areas of common ground. A successful mediation effort has a conflict negotiation as an outcome, which is accepted and owned by the parties themselves.

Five basic principles support great conflict negotiation skills:

- Be hard on the problem and soft on the person

- Be inventive about options

- Emphasize common ground

- Focus on needs, not positions

- Make clear agreements

Conflict negotiators should commit to a win/win approach, even if tactics used by the other person seem unfair. Clarify right up front that your task will be to guide the negotiation in a positive direction. In doing so, you may have to adopt some of these strategies:

- **Reframe** – You may ask a party in the conflict to reframe a point of view, or you may reframe it yourself and ask for a feedback. For instance, you may ask the parties what would happen if you (all of you, not only you!) were to succeed in resolving the conflict, what differences would they notice?

- **Address the issue, do not overreact** – This is very important! Make sure you:

  - Overlook accusations, attacks, threats or ultimatums.

  - Allow the other parties to back down without feeling humiliated or defeated. No "I told you so!!"

- Manage your emotions.

- **Stay with the issue** - Maintain the relationship and try to resolve the issue. If necessary summarize how far you all have gotten. Identify common ground and agreements established so far. Focus on being partners solving the problem, not opponents. Break it down, divide the conflict into parts. Divide and conquer!

- **No tolerance for unfair tactics** – Decide that proper behavior during the conflict negotiation will be the tactic to be used. Do not accept unfair behavior, or tactics.

Establish a Conducive Environment for Conflict Negotiation

The base for any effort to collaboratively negotiate conflicts is an affirming environment. By developing such environment you should foster an improved sense of trust, integrity, security, and safety for the negotiation process. By doing so, you significantly improve the likelihood of initiatives to solve conflicts to be reciprocated. In many ways, we must accept as a point of departure that the relationship between the parties is not filled with trust, at least vis-à-vis the situation, and its immediate threat. Therefore, two options present themselves:

- Build a sense of trust as a first priority;

- Accept that we lack trust, and practically consider how to work together in spite of it.

In practice, there are several useful strategies that can be brought to bear on this challenge:

1. **Identify the fear** - By naming the fear, its sources and its triggers, we free ourselves to put that issue on the table and address its influence on other issues of impasse, especially substantive needs.

2. **Establish ground rules** - This is often an important strategy for clarifying expectations about procedural needs and psychological needs in negotiation.

3. **Engage in an appreciative inquiry** – This is the process that focuses on what has gone right in the past, and what we wish to bring forward as key themes and values for the future. This approach turns the conflict on its head. By reframing the situation to focus on positive elements, participants may be able to successfully shift from adversarial orientations to problem-solving attitudes. It is also surprising to opponents when such an approach diffuses the energy that otherwise would be going into sustaining the framework of conflict.

4. **Understanding the meaning of a specific conflict** - Addressing specific concerns cannot be done in a vacuum; they must be understood within the context that they are occurring. When viewing the opportunity to build an affirming environment, it also challenges us to develop workplace systems that are respectful, consistent, filled with integrity and positively reinforcing

5. **It takes courage to resolve conflicts** - Engaging in a dispute resolution requires courage. It requires us to confront and acknowledge our fears, and face the threats embedded in the conflict that we often would prefer not to acknowledge.

Attitudes for Conflict Resolution Mediators

These attitudes are relevant in a conflict resolution where you are the mediator, such as in a formally organized mediation session.

1. Be objective, by validating both sides

2. Be supportive, by using reconciliatory language. Provide a non-threatening learning environment

3. Don't judge, by actively discouraging judgments as to who was right, and who was wrong. The issue is not about who's right, but what is right. Don't ask "Why did you?" Ask "What happened?" and "How did you feel?"

4. Guide the process, do not direct, by using astute questioning, such as encouraging suggestions from the parties involved, being silent, resisting advising

5. Foster a win/win situation, by working towards wins for both sides. Turn opponents into problem-solving partners.

Chapter 8
Conflict Resolution Best Practices

"A man will fight harder for his interests than for his rights."[1]

By Marcia Valeria Goncalves[2]

Overview

At this stage in the book it is understood that conflicts will always occur, both at the professional and personal levels. It is, therefore, important to have ways to deal with these conflicts and accept them as part of any environment, especially the professional one, as conflicts can be catalysts for creativity and innovation, and not something negative to be avoided.

Throughout this book we discuss the origins of conflicts, why they happen, how to deal with them, and how to mediate more serious ones. In this next-to-last chapter we will look into some tools and techniques to assist you in more effectively dealing with conflicts, whether you are self-mediating or mediating a group.

The dynamics and techniques found here are traditionally used for conflict resolution, but are not guaranteed to always work. Some dynamics and techniques can produce very positive results, while others, unfortunately, may produce negative ones, or may even exacerbating the conflict. As previously discussed, mediators are not always successful in mediating a conflict.

This chapter, therefore, attempts to provide a list of best practices for dealing with conflicts, taking also into consideration the

---

[1] Napoleon Bonaparte
[2] Professor of Management at Faculdades Estacio de Sa, Vitoria-ES, Brazil.

multidimensional aspects that impact conflicts and that are impacted by them.

Best Practices for Mediating Conflicts

In becoming a successful conflict mediator (or self-mediator), there are several areas you will need to focus on. Throughout this book we have looked into personal and professionals attributes you must cultivate and acquire when dealing with conflict resolution. The following are other business, logistic and strategic issues you should be aware of.

Business Needs Must be Isolated

You must have a clear business goal in mind before attempting to mediate any conflict among multiple parties (i.e. teams, multi-party conflicts, interdepartmental, conflict with clients). Whatever strategy you choose, you must keep in mind the return on investment, it must affect the bottom line. While appeasing issues between coworkers is a good strategy overall, it will only make sense when business is suffering. Invariably you will need to do an evaluation based on how your organization operates its current business

Strategic Orientation

Strategic orientation is very important if you want conflict resolution strategies to succeed. It all starts with communication, which is the organization's lifeblood, in enabling and energizing employees to carry out the strategic intent of a conflict resolution culture. I say culture because, to be effective and help any organization to succeed in resolving their conflicts you will need the capability of rapidly identifying, sending, receiving, and understanding strategic information circulating amongst the parties in conflict, to verify if it is credible, sensible, and relevant.

However, in today's dynamic organizations, you will need more than successfully executing a conflict resolution strategy, or bringing about a culture of change. You will need a broad awareness, understanding and acceptance of strategic intent by all people in the organization, their willingness to always strive to resolve their conflicts, as a foundation of their commitment.

Therefore, decisions on conflict resolution strategies (and training!) and policy must take into account the imperative and the challenge of communication, and the tools and talent of the communication function must be oriented to the organization's conflict resolution priorities.

Aim for Integrity

All communications should be credible. To be credible, the communication needs to have integrity, and only constant and complete consistency between communication and conduct can deliver that in a conflicting environment. Thus, make sure to demonstrate integrity as a mentor, or if you are part of the conflict, as someone who is honest and fair. Always take into account an organization's formal, semi-formal, and informal voices.

The rhetoric by which an organization manages its affairs and presents itself to others is manifestly important in conflict resolution, but its impact as communication is never equal to or greater than that of the organization's decisions and actions. In other words, always do what you say you will do. For through such decisions and actions, an organization continually refines and defines itself.

Only through mutual dignity and respect will conflict resolution best practices thrive. Organizations that are blessed by such relationships will, over time, develop greater internal commitment to resolving conflicts and thus outperform and surpass organizations that are not. An organization's success ultimately depends on the fully aligned, discretionary, principled, and inspired effort of its people. Conflict resolutions based on mutual dignity and respect is the foundation of such efforts, and therefore critical to the success of the organization.

Get Strategic Information Flowing

The flow of strategic information, as depicted in Figure 8.1, enriches and empowers an organization when dealing with conflicts. It must nurture and sustain the systematic flow of credible, sensible, timely, and relevant information in order to bring all their resources to bear on the execution of its strategic intent. That requires the full commitment of leadership, the application of appropriate conflict resolution styles, and the broad participation and support of employees, and all parties involved in the conflict.

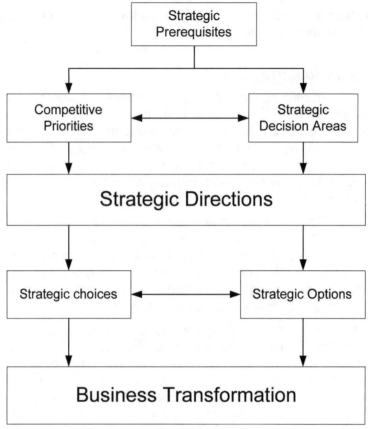

Figure 8.1 – Strategic information flow assists in the conflict resolution process

Leadership's support of upward flow of information is critical. Leadership must be receptive to upward thrusts, especially when mediators deal with negative information, as it is a reflection of the trust it holds in the staff. The flow of strategic information through an organization is a barometer of its ability to resolve conflicts, regardless of the kind of information flowing.

During Conflict Resolution, Messages must be Clear and Powerful

Unless your communication is clear, you might as well not attempt to communicate or mediate a conflict, otherwise you may end up confusing people, leading them to complacency or generating false expectations, even chaos, which could be very detrimental to the conflict. Therefore, when mediating conflicts, make sure to do so with simplicity, and not complexity; with an economy of words, but a wealth of meaning. The language should be plain English, such as used in everyday conversation, free of jargon and technicalities.

Communicating through parables or stories is often very powerful in conflict resolution sessions, as it usually addresses the concerns and needs of listeners, and naturally takes the form of a conversation, more than a lecture or an announcement would. In addition, make sure to communicate clearly and powerfully through messages that are coherent, consistent, and complete. Make sure to acknowledge the limits of the stories(?), explain their rationale, and speak to whatever questions they may have raised.

The Power of Listening

Listening involves hearing, sensing, interpretation, evaluation and response. Good listening is an essential part of being a good mediator, and the cornerstone of conflict resolution strategies. You cannot be a good mediator unless you are a good listener. As mediator, you must be very aware of the feedback you are receiving from the people around you. If you are not a good listener, your future as a conflict mediator will be limited.

Good listening includes a range of skills, including knowledge of technique and practice that is very similar to good writing or good speaking. In fact, poor listening skills are more common than poor speaking skills. I am sure that you have seen on many occasions, two or more people talking to each other at the same time.

In improving your listening skills, be aware that there is shallow listening and deep listening. Shallow or superficial listening is all too common in business settings and many other settings. Most of us have learned how to give the appearance of listening to our supervisors, the public speaker, and the chair of the meeting while not really listening. Even less obvious is when the message received is different from the one sent. We did not really understand what the message is. We listened, but we did not get the intended message. Such failed communications are the consequences of poor speaking, poor listening and/or poor understanding.

Figure 8.2 illustrates the eight levels of listening, varying from *ignoring*, or not listening at all to what is being said, up through *generating*, which is a complete and undivided attention to what is being said that may actually encourage or generate exceptional behavior by the speaker.. Beyond that is the peak of the mountain, which represents the *mastery* you can achieve in the ability to listen to other people while you are speaking. Try and imagine times when you thought you were listening to an opponent but you were really projecting. Think of a time when someone thanked you for listening to his or her words and ideas. Go back to past conversations that left you feeling disempowered, frustrated or resigned. What worked and what did not in the way you were listening or being listened to.

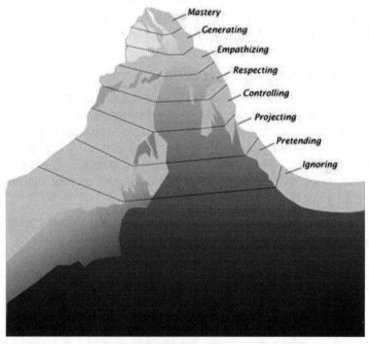

Figure 8.2 – Strategic information flow assists in the conflict resolution process

Figure 8.2 breaks down the ability any party in a conflict has to listen in seven levels:

1. **Ground Zero is Ignoring**, or the absence of listening. When we ignore a person's idea or request during conflict mediation, we contribute to that person's resignation and loss of spirit. Ignoring is rampant in organizations and can have real opportunity costs, from loss of morale to brain drain to severe conflicts and lawsuits.

2. **Level One is Pretending** to listen or ignoring with the added dimension of hypocrisy. People who pretend to be listening at least realize that they should be listening, although they are clearly busy with other activities.

3. **Level Two is Controlling** or listening in such a way that influences what the speaker has to say—through gestures, facial expressions or sounds. Authority figures such as senior executives, judges, professors and doctors often have a controlling level of listening, even if that person has no intention of controlling what the participants said.

4. **Level Three is Projecting**, or responding to your own interpretation of what is being or has been said, rather than what the member in a conflict is actually trying to convey. Because each one of us views the world through a different filter (remember the discussion about perceptions?), we all project in our listening in some way. This is not a powerful way of listening because it is selective and you are not hearing the other party fully.

5. **Level Four is Respecting** or hearing the content of the communication, nothing more, nothing less. You are not thinking about what you are going to say next and you are giving the speaker your complete and undivided attention.

6. **Level Five is Empathizing,** which requires seeing things from the conflict member's point of view by standing in their shoes and hearing the intention beneath the conflict. When we are able to understand where a person is coming from, we can hear their intentions more clearly.

7. **Level Six is Generating**, one of the highest levels of listening as it evokes the best qualities in others. When we listen to

101

others in a conflict as the powerful beings that they are, we can actually encourage their brilliance.

8. **Level Seven is Mastery** or the ability to shape how others in a conflict listen to you. Powerful leaders, or mediators (yes, they are leaders!) who have reached this level of listening are actually able to let the parties in a conflict speak through them by giving voice to their unspoken thoughts and wishes.

Listening skills can always be improved. Perfection in listening, just as in other communications skills, does not exist. There are several good books and many articles on good listening. In addition to the eight levels described above, there are also three basic listening modes: combative, attentive and reflective. Most of us would describe our listening as attentive, that we are interested in the other person's point of view. I have had many departmental managers come up to me in a combative mode when involved in conflicts. They clearly did not want to hear my explanations, but wanted to promote theirs. All too seldom do we take the reflective mode in which we take an active role in the communications process to resolve conflicts. We are not just passive vessels into which information is poured, but we ought to think critically about the topics and the messages we receive.

The following attributes of good listening are suggestive of the skills needed for becoming a good conflict mediator; there is some overlap between the various attributes, but each suggests something different:

- **Attention** - Attention may be defined as the visual portion of concentration on the speaker. Through eye contact and other body language, we communicate to the speaker that we are paying close attention to his/her messages. All the same time we are reading the verbal and nonverbal cues from the speaker, the speaker is reading ours. What messages are we sending out? If we lean forward a little and focus our eyes on the person, the message is we are paying close attention.

- **Concentration** - Good listening is normally hard work. At every moment we are receiving literally millions of sensory messages. Nerve endings on our bottom are telling us the chair is hard, others are saying our clothes are binding, nerve ending in our nose are picking up the smells of cooking

French fries or whatever, our ears are hearing the buzzing of the computer fan, street sounds, music in the background and dozens of other sounds, our emotions are reminding us of that fight we had with our mate last night, and thousands more signals are knocking at the doors of our senses. Focus your attention on the words, ideas and feeling related to the subject. Concentrate on the main ideas or points. Don't let examples or fringe comments distract you.

- **Don't Interject** - There is a great temptation at many times for the listener to jump in and say in essence: "isn't this really what you meant to say." This carries the message: "I can say it better than you can," which stifles any further messages from the speaker. Often, this process may degenerate into a game of one-upmanship in which each person tries to outdo the other and very little communication occurs.

- **Empathy** - not sympathy - Empathy is the action of actively understanding, being aware of, being sensitive to, and vicariously experiencing the feelings, thoughts, and experience of another. Sympathy is sharing common feelings. In other words as a good listener you need to be able to understand the other person, you do not have to become like them. Try to put yourself in the speaker's position so that you can see what he/she is trying to get at.

- **Eye contact** - Good eye contact is essential for several reasons. By maintaining eye contact, some of the competing visual inputs are eliminated. You are not as likely to be distracted from the person talking to you. Another reason, most of us have learned to read lips, often unconsciously, and the lip reading helps us to understand verbal messages. Also, much of many messages are in non-verbal form and by watching the eyes and face of a person we pick up clues as to the content. A squinting of the eyes may indicate close attention. A slight nod indicates understanding or agreement. Verbal messages may have several meanings, depending upon voice inflection, voice modulation, facial expression, etc.

- **Leave the Channel Open** - A good listener always leaves open the possibility of additional messages. A brief question or a nod will often encourage additional communications

- **Objective** - We should be open to the message the other person is sending. It is very difficult to be completely open because each of us is strongly biased by the weight of our past experiences. We give meaning to the the words and symbols of the messages based upon what we have been taught by our parents, our peers and our teachers. Talk to someone from a different culture and watch how they give meaning to words. Another listening challenge is to listen openly and objectively to a person with very different political or religious beliefs. Can you do that? You have a tremendous talent if you can, but relatively few people can listen, understand and appreciate messages that are very different from their own. If you cannot, it is time to start because as a leader, you will need to understand a wide range of opinions on often-controversial subjects.

- **Receptive Body Language** - Certain body postures and movements are culturally interpreted with specific meanings. The crossing of arms and legs is perceived to mean a closing of the mind and attention. The nodding of the head vertically is interpreted as agreement or assent. Now, be careful, as nonverbal clues such as these vary from culture to culture just as the spoken language does. If seated, the leaning forward with the upper body communicates attention. Standing or seated, the maintenance of an appropriate distance is important. Too close and we appear to be pushy or aggressive; too far and we are seen as cold.

- **Restating the message** - Your restating the message as part of the feedback can enhance the effectiveness of good communications. Make a comment such as: "I want to make sure that I have fully understood your message.....," and then paraphrase the message in your own words. If the communication is not clear, such a feedback will allow for immediate clarification. It is important that you state the message as clearly and objectively as possible.

- **Strategic Pauses** - Pauses can be used very effectively in listening. For example, pauses at some points in the feedback can be used to signal that you are carefully considering the message--that you are "thinking" about what was just said.

- **Understanding of Communication Symbols** - A good command of the spoken language is essential in good listening. Meaning must be imputed to the words. For many common words in the English language there are multiple meanings. The three-letter word, "run" has more than a hundred different uses. You as the listener must concentrate on the context of the usage in order to correctly understand the message. The spoken portion of the language is only a fraction of the message. Voice inflection, body language and other symbols send messages also. Thus, a considerable knowledge of nonverbal language is important in good listening.

- **You cannot listen while you are talking** - This is very obvious, but very frequently overlooked or ignored. An important question to ask is: Why are you talking? Is it to draw attention to yourself?

In summary, good listening is more than polite silence and attention when others speak, and it's altogether different from manipulative tactics masquerading as skills. Rather, it is a high virtue, a value, a reflection of bedrock belief that learning what other people have on their minds is a wise investment of one's time. It requires intellectual humility and the willingness to learn from people from all stations of life. In addition to learning, good listening also establishes a welcoming rapport that builds relationships of respect and dignity, conducive to frequent, candid and rapid communication.

Communication Structure and Process

The structure and process of internal communication should reflect the fact that communication is a means, not an end, to success. The fundamental purpose of workplace communication is to enhance the business performance of the organization. Communication succeeds only to the extent that it enables and energizes employees to align their work with the organization's strategic intent.

A preoccupation with artistry or diction in communications may divert attention away from the conflict resolution process. The responsibility and tools for strategic communication should be distributed throughout the organization, so that each employee is an integral part of the process. The communication function should foster alliances with the management teams of operating units. Given a choice between centralizing and decentralizing the communication function, the latter affords more regular contact with line managers, which in turn builds mutual understanding between line and staff functions.

Evaluating Your Systems

Measurement is a vital aspect of a high-performance system of strategic workplace communication, but it must be undertaken with care and skill. It is a myth that everything of importance in organizations can be measured; integrity, perseverance, teamwork, agility and other essential attributes of a vital work culture all but defy measurement.

The importance or value of strategic communication is not an appropriate subject for measurement; by definition, it is always and precisely dependent upon the value of the strategy or the change or the goal that it supports. Nor are the tactical and mundane aspects of communication a worthwhile focus of measurement. Rather, the measurement of communication must concentrate on its effectiveness with respect to strategic direction—whether it adapts to changing circumstances, engages management in the essential tasks of leadership communication, establishes a basis for accountability, and charts organizational progress.

The best measurement processes address not only formal communication but also semi-formal and informal communication. They focus on outcomes, not on outputs or inputs. They measure a progression of awareness, understanding, acceptance, and commitment, and they reflect the fundamental purpose of communication as a bridge between strategy and its successful execution.

Planning as a Tool for Conflict Resolution

One of the most efficient tools for dealing with conflicts is the preventive planning approach. Its objective is to generate conflicts that are beneficial or functional to the organization or corporation, in place of dysfunctional conflicts that tend to disrupt the performance of the organization and are much harder to deal with. So, keep in mind: conflicts can be good!

Functional conflicts can help the performance of a team in a constructive way. There are three types of conflict planning that have the potential to preempt any destructive effects of a conflict at an organization, including:

- **Technical planning** – There are certain functions in the organization that tend to generate conflicts, such as human resources, planning, and execution of projects. If such functions are managed appropriately, the chance of conflicts being generated is minimized.

- **Integration planning** – We know that to integrate a group is one of the most difficult tasks in any professional (or social) organization. The more we attempt to integrate a group or draw closer to an individual (whether in a professional or social setting) the more conflicting the interaction becomes. The conflicts can vary from clashes of interests, anxieties and frustration, to power struggles with the status quo and other habits. These conflicts can also be managed by planning ahead. An integration plan, where teams and new additions to those teams are well thought out, can dramatically decrease the number of conflicts.

- **Planning process** – To plan how to manage (and mediate) conflicts you first need to create a process of how each planning sequence will work. It is important to analyze how the process will be developed and who will be part of this process

Good conflict mediators prefer to deal with conflict at its early stages. It is a lot easier to identify the differences and points of conflict at the beginning, when it is easier to separate the emotional from the actual issues, rather than later on. Tangible barriers can be removed at this stage and you are more likely to succeed in the mediation process.

Chapter 9
Test Yourself: Are You a Good Conflict Mediator?

"It is easier to fight for one's principles than to live up to them."[1]

Take this small test below to assess if you are, or could be, a good conflict mediator. This test[2] also helps you assess how well you are able to self-mediate your conflicts. Select True (T) or False (F) for each statement below, and then review your results after you are done.

Are You a Good Conflict Mediator?

1. All conflicts can be resolved. T or F?

2. Conflicts almost always end up in a winner and a loser. T or F?

3. Inasmuch as we don't want to accept it, conflicts are inevitable at organizations. T or F?

4. The goals and interests of employees and coworkers are often in conflict with the organizations. T or F?

5. If the goals of a person or group interfere with the goals of another person or group, it is certain that there will be a conflict. T or F?

---

[1] Alfred Adler
[2] Berg, 2006

6. The behavior demonstrated by an employee can be a visible expression of a hidden feeling or emotion. T or F?

7. Above all, a supervisor should make sure that his team is happy. T or F?

8. Acknowledging to a subordinate that you were wrong can weaken your position as his or her supervisor. T or F?

9. After giving a chance to someone in a conflict to express his or her issues, a mediator (or supervisor) should collect as much information as possible regarding the issue, instead of making a quick decision. T or F?

10. Preconcepts and discriminations (i.e. based on sex, race, religion, color, age, etc.) are some of the main filters guiding our perceptions, judgments and attitudes. T or F?

11. As a team leader, to lose your patience with your team every now and then can help maintain discipline and improve productivity. T or F?

12. When mediating conflicts, the most important thing is to be abreast of the facts and solutions, and not the personalities and behaviors of the parties involved. T or F?

13. It is most important is to make sure that your department is productive and efficient, even if the strategy interferes or jeopardizes the work of other departments at the organization. T or F?

14. If avoided or ignored, conflicts may very well disappear. T or F?

15. It is more important to be competent and do a job well, than interact well with the coworkers. T or F?

16. Tranquility is a receptive posture, and often disarms aggressive attitudes in a conflict. T or F?

17. We should never interrupt a person when he or she is sharing their opinions. T or F?

18. Conflicts among your team should always be resolved right away. T or F?

19. Sometimes, when there is a necessity to implement unpopular decisions, it is not necessary to negotiate it with the people involved. T or F?

20. Conflicts can help foster relationships. T or F?

21. All and every type of conflict in an organization must be resolved. T or F?

22. The moment and the environment influence tremendously the result, favorable or not, of a conflict. T or F?

Evaluate Yourself

Add up your points only to the following questions:

- Add one (1) point for every statement from the statements listed below that you answered True (T):

    3, 5, 6, 9, 10, 12, 16, 9, 20, 22.

- Add one (1) point for every statement listed below that you answered False (F):

    1, 2, 4, 7, 8, 11, 13, 14, 15, 17, 18, 21.

Evaluation Criteria

- **From 20 to 22 points** – You are a very good conflict mediator and know when and how to confront situations that are really problematic. Congratulations!!

- **From 16 to 19 points** – You are a good conflict mediator and are able to perceive the conflicts at hand. There is room for improvement though!

- **From 12 to 15 points** – Your points are average. Often you are able to achieve good results in mediating conflicts, but other times you tend to commit mistakes that can become very problematic.

- **Below 12 points** – You need to improve dramatically your ability to mediate conflicts. Probably you often do not recognize conflicts and behaviors that can be better dealt with in their early stages. Try to learn more about conflict resolution (above and beyond this quick guide!), and to practice it in your day-to-day work.

Questions to Reflect

1. Do you think that competition and conflict are different things? Explain.

2. What can you do to improve you effectiveness as a negotiator?

3. What are the techniques for conflict resolution?

References and Recommended Reading

Avruch, K., P. Black, and J. Scimecca. 1991. Conflict Resolution: Cross-Cultural Perspectives. New York: Greenwood Press.

Axelrod, Robert. 1984. The Evolution of Cooperation. New York: Basic Books.

Azar, Edward E., and John W. Burton. 1986. International Conflict Resolution: Theory and Practice. Boulder: Lynne Rienner Publishers.

Bercovitch, Jacob. 1991. "International Mediation and Dispute Settlement: Evaluating the Conditions for Successful Mediation." Negotiation Journal 7(1):17-30.

Bondurant, Joan V. 1965. Conquest of Violence: The Gandhian Philosophy of Conflict. Berkeley: University of California Press.

Boulding, Elise, Clovis Brigagao, and Kevin Clements. 1991. Peace Culture and Society: Transnational Research and Dialogue. Boulder: Westview Press.

Boulding, Elise. 1990. Building a Global Civic Culture: Education for an Interdependent World. Syracuse, NY: Syracuse University Press.

Boulding, Kenneth. 1962. Conflict and Defense: A General Theory. New York: Harper Torchbooks.

Boulding, Kenneth. 1978a. Ecodynamics: A New Theory of Societal Evolution. Beverly Hills, CA: Sage.

Boulding, Kenneth. 1978b. Stable Peace. Austin: University of Texas Press.

Boulding, Kenneth. 1985. Human Betterment. Beverly Hills, CA: Sage.

Boulding, Kenneth. 1989. Three Faces of Power. Newbury Park, CA: Sage Publications.

Boutros-Ghali, Boutros. 1995. An Agenda for Development. New York: United Nations.

Boutros-Ghali, Boutros. 1995. An Agenda for Peace, with the new supplement and related UN documents. New York: United Nations..

Burton, John W. 1989. "On the Need for Conflict Prevention." Center for Conflict Analysis and Resolution, George Mason University, Fairfax, VA.

Burton, John, and Frank Dukes, eds. 1990b. Conflict: Readings in Management and Resolution. New York: St.

Burton, John, and Frank Dukes. 1990a. "Conflict: Practices in Management, Settlement and Resolution." In Community Mediation. New York: St. Martin's Press.

Burton, John. 1987. Resolving Deep-Rooted Conflict: A Handbook. Lanham, MD: University Press of America.

Burton, John. 1990a. Conflict: Human Needs Theory. New York: St. Martin's Press.

Bush, Robert A. Baruch, and Joseph P. Folger. 1994. Promise of Mediation. San Francisco: Jossey-Bass.

Butfoy, Andrew. 1993. "Collective Security: Theory, Problems and Reformulations." Australian Journal of International Affairs 47:1-14.

Carpenter, Susan L., and W. J. D. Kennedy. 1988. Managing Public Disputes. San Francisco: Jossey-Bass.

Carter, Jimmy. 1982. Keeping Faith: Memoirs of a President. New York: Bantam Books.

Casse, Pierre and Surinder Deol. 1985. Managing Intercultural Negotiations. Washington D.C.: Sietar International.

Cohen, Raymond. 1996. "Cultural Aspects of International Mediation." In Resolving International Conflicts: The Theory and Practice of Mediation (pp. 107-25), edited by Jacob Bercovitch. Boulder: Lynne Rienner Publishers.

Corbin, Jane. 1994. The Norway Channel: The Secret Talks that Led to the Middle East Peace Accord. New York: Atlantic Monthly Press.

Curle, Adam. 1986. In the Middle: Non-official Mediation in Violent Situations. New York: St. Martins Press.

Deutsch, Morton. 1973. The Resolution of Conflict: Constructive and Destructive Processes. New Haven, CT: Yale University Press.

Diamond, Louise, and John McDonald. 1991. Multi-Track Diplomacy: A Systems Guide and Analysis. Grinnell: Iowa Peace Institute.

Evans, Gareth. 1993. Cooperating for Peace: The Global Agenda for the 1990s and Beyond. Sydney, Australia: Allen and Unwin.

Farson, R. (1997). Management of the Absurd: Paradoxes in Leadership, Simon & Schuster, New York, NY.

Fisher, Roger, and Scott Brown. 1988. Getting Together: Building a Relationship that Gets to Yes. Boston: Houghton Mifflin.

Fisher, Roger, and William Ury. Getting to Yes. New York: Penguin Books.

Fisher, Roger, Elizabeth Kopelman, and Andrea Kupfer Schneider. 1994. Beyond Machiavelli: Tools for Coping with Conflict. Cambridge: Harvard University Press.

Fisher, Roger, William Ury, and Bruce Patton. 1991. Getting to Yes, 2nd ed. New York: Penguin Books.

Fisher, Roger. 1991. Beyond YES. Cambridge: Program on Negotiation at Harvard Law School.

Fisher, Roger. 1994. "In Theory Deter, Compel, or Negotiate?" Negotiation Journal 10:17-32.

Folberg, Jay, and Alison Taylor. 1984. Mediation: A Comprehensive Guide to Resolving Conflicts without Litigation. San Francisco: Jossey-Bass.

Folger, Joseph P., and Marshall Scott Poole. 1984. Working through Conflict: A Communication Perspective. Glenview, IL: Scott, Foresman.

Galtung, Johan. 1995. Choose Peace. East Haven, CT: Pluto Press.

Galtung, Johan. 1996. Peace by Peaceful Means. Thousand Oaks, CA: Sage Publications.

Gandhi, Mohandas K. 1971. "Non-Violence." In Civil Disobedience and Violence, edited by Jeffrie G. Murphy. Belmont, CA: Wadsworth Publishing Co.

Goldberg, Stephen B., Eric D. Green, and Frank E. A. Sander. 1985. Dispute Resolution. Boston: Little, Brown.

Goldberg, Stephen B., Frank E. A. Sander, and Nancy H. Rogers. 1992. Dispute Resolution: Negotiation, Mediation, and Other Processes. Boston: Little, Brown.

Gray, Barbara. 1989. Collaborating: Finding Common Ground for Multiparty Problems. San Francisco: Jossey-Bass.

Green, Martin Burgess. 1986. The Origins of Nonviolence: Tolstoy and Gandhi in Their Historical Settings. University Park: Pennsylvania State University Press.

Gregg, Richard B. 1966. The Power of Nonviolence. New York: Schocken Books.

Gurr, Ted R. 1970. Why Men Rebel. Princeton, NJ: Princeton University Press.

Gurr, Ted Robert, and Barbara Harff. 1994. Ethnic Conflict in World Politics. Boulder: Westview Press.

Handy, C. (1995). The Age of Paradox, Harvard Business School Press, Cambridge, MA.

Hankins, Gary. 1988. Prescription for Anger. Beaverton, OR: Princess Publishing.

Hardin, Garrett. 1968. "The Tragedy of the Commons." Science 162:1243.

Kelman, Herbert, and Stephen Cohen. 1976. "The Problem-Solving Workshop: A Social Psychological Contribution to the Resolution of Conflict." Journal of Peace Research 8(2):79-90.

King, Martin Luther Jr. 1964. Why We Can't Wait. New York: Harper and Row.

King, Martin Luther Jr. 1967. Where Do We Go from Here: Chaos or Community? New York: Harper and Row.

King, Martin Luther Jr. 1983. "`I Have a Dream" Speech Given on August 28, 1963." In The Words of Martin Luther King, Jr., edited by Coretta Scott King. New York: Newmarket Press.

Kolb, Deborah M., and Associates. 1994. When Talk Works: Profiles of Mediators. San Francisco: Jossey-Bass.

Korda, M. (2000). Another Life, Delta, New York, NY.

Kremenyuk, V.A. (ed.) 1991. International Negotiation: Analysis, Approaches, and Issues. San Francisco: Jossey-Bass.

Kriesberg, Louis, and Stuart J. Thorson. 1991. Timing the De-escalation of International Conflicts. Syracuse, NY: Syracuse University Press.

Kriesberg, Louis, Terrell A. Northrup, and Stuart J. Thorson. 1989. Intractable Conflicts and Their Transformation. Syracuse, NY: Syracuse University Press.

Kriesberg, Louis. 1998. Constructive Conflict. NY: Rowman and Littlefield.

Larson, Carl E., and David D. Chrislip. 1994. Collaborative Leadership. San Francisco: Jossey-Bass.

Lederach, John Paul. 1995. Preparing for Peace: Conflict Transformation Across Cultures. Syracuse, NY: Syracuse University Press.

Lederach, John Paul. 1998. Building Peace: Sustainable Reconciliation in Divided Societies. Washington D.C., U.S. Institute of Peace Press

Lindblom, Charles E. 1968. The Policy-Making Process. Englewood Cliffs, NJ: Prentice Hall.

Mayer, B. (2000). The Dynamics of Conflict Resolution: A Practitioner's Guide, John Wiley & Son, New York-NY.

Merwe, Hugo van der, and Dennis J. D. Sandole. 1993. Conflict Resolution Theory and Practice: Integration and Application. New York: Manchester University Press..

Mitchell, C. R. 1991. "A Willingness to Talk: Conciliatory Gestures and De-Escalation." Negotiation Journal 7(4):405-29.

Mitchell, C. R. 1993. "Track Two Triumphant? Reflections on the Oslo Process and Conflict Resolution in the Middle East." ICAR Newsletter 5(6):8, 12.

Montville, Joseph. 1987. "The Arrow and the Olive Branch: A Case for Track Two Diplomacy." In Conflict Resolution: Track Two Diplomacy, edited by J. McDonald and D. Bendahmane. Washington, DC: Foreign Service Institute, U.S. Department of State.

Montville, Joseph. 1990. Conflict and Peacemaking In Multiethnic Societies. Lexington, MA and Toronto: Lexington Books.

Montville, Joseph. 1993. "The Healing Function in Political Conflict Resolution." In Conflict Resolution Theory and Practice: Integration and Application, edited by Dennis J. D. Sandole and Hugo van der Merwe. New York: Manchester University Press.

Moore, Christopher W. 1966. The Mediation Process, Second Edition. San Francisco: Jossey-Bass.

Moore, Christopher W. 1986. The Mediation Process. San Francisco: Jossey-Bass.

Newhouse, John. 1989. War and Peace in the Nuclear Age. New York: Knopf.

Northrup, Terrell A. 1989. "Dynamic of Identity." In Intractable Conflicts and Their Transformation, edited by Louis Kriesberg, Terrell A. Northrup, and Stuart J. Thorson. Syracuse, NY: Syracuse University Press.

Olczak, Paul V., and Dean G. Pruitt. 1995. "Beyond Hope: Approaches to Resolving Seemingly Intractable Conflict." In Conflict, Cooperation and Justice: Essays Inspired by the Work of Morton Deutsch, edited by Barbara Benedict Bunker, Jeffrey Z. Rubin, and associates. San Francisco: Jossey-Bass.

Olson, David. 1980. The Legislative Process: A Comparative Approach. New York: Harper and Row.

Osgood, Charles E. 1962. An Alternative to War or Surrender. Urbana: University of Illinois Press.

Osgood, Charles E. 1966. Perspective in Foreign Policy. Palo Alto, CA: Pacific Books.

Raiffa, Howard. 1982. The Art and Science of Negotiation. Cambridge: Belknap Press of Harvard University Press.

Rapoport, Anatol, ed. 1974. Game Theory as a Theory of Conflict Resolution. Boston. D. Reidel Publishing.

Rapoport, Anatol. 1960. Fights, Games, and Debates. Ann Arbor: University of Michigan Press.

Richardson, Lewis F. 1960. Arms and Insecurity. Pittsburgh, PA: Boxwood Press.

Richardson, Lewis F. 1960. Statistics of Deadly Quarrels. Chicago: Quadrangle Books.

Ross, Marc H. The Culture of Conflict. New Haven: Yale University Press, 1993.

Rothman, Jay. 1992. Confrontation to Cooperation: Resolving Ethnic and Regional Conflict. Newbury Park, CA: Sage Publications.

Rothman, Jay. 1997. Resolving Identity Conflicts in Nations, Organizations, and Communities. San Francisco: Jossey-Bass.

Ryan, Stephen. 1995. Ethnic Conflict and International Relations. Brookfield, VT: Dartmouth.

Sandole, Dennis J. D., and Hugo van der Merwe, eds. 1993. Conflict Resolution Theory and Practice: Integration and Application. New York: Manchester University Press.

Schelling, Thomas C. 1960. Strategy of Conflict. Cambridge: Harvard

Sharp, Gene, and Bruce Jenkins. 1990. Civilian-Based Defense: A Post-Military Weapons System. Princeton, NJ: Princeton University Press.

Sharp, Gene. 1973. The Politics of Nonviolent Action. Boston: Porter Sargent.

Susskind, Lawrence, and Jeffrey Cruikshank. 1987. Breaking the Impasse. New York: Basic Books.

Susskind, Lawrence, and Patrick Field. 1996. Dealing with an Angry Public. New York: Free Press.

Tillet, Gregory. 1991. Resolving Conflict: A Practical Approach. Sydney, Australia: Sydney University Press.

Touval, Saadia, and I. William Zartman. 1985. International Mediation in Theory and Practice. Boulder: Westview Press.

Touval, Saadia. 1995. "Ethical Dilemmas in International Mediation." Negotiation Journal 11:333-38.

Umbreit, Mark S. 1995. Mediating Interpersonal Conflicts: A Pathway to Peace. West Concord, MN: CPI Publishing.

United Nations. 1992. Handbook on the Peaceful Settlement of Disputes between States. New York: United

Ury, William L. 1985. Beyond the Hotline: How Crisis Control Can Prevent Nuclear War. Boston: Houghton Mifflin.

Ury, William L., Jeanne M. Brett, and Stephen B. Goldberg. 1988a. Getting Disputes Resolved: Designing Systems to Cut the Costs of Conflict. San Francisco: Jossey-Bass.

Ury, William. 1991. Getting Past No: Negotiating with Difficult People. New York: Bantam Books.

Vogele, William B. 1993. "Deterrence by Civilian Defense." Peace and Change 18:1:26-49.

Wehr, Paul, Heidi Burgess, and Guy Burgess. 1994. Justice without Violence. Boulder: Lynne Rienner Publishers.

Zartman, I. William. 1985. Ripe for Resolution. New York: Oxford University Press.